The King's Wages

Augustine Brempong

Langaa Research & Publishing CIG
Mankon, Bamenda

Publisher:

Langaa RPCIG
Langaa Research & Publishing Common Initiative Group
P.O. Box 902 Mankon
Bamenda
North West Region
Cameroon
Langaagrp@gmail.com
www.langaa-rpcig.net

Distributed in and outside N. America by African Books Collective
orders@africanbookscollective.com
www.africanbookscollective.com

ISBN: 9956-762-01-6

DISCLAIMER
All views expressed in this publication are those of the author and do
not necessarily reflect the views of Langaa RPCIG.

About the Author

Augustine Brempong was born in the city of Kumasi, Ghana, on 16 June 1988. At an early age, he developed an immense interest in storytelling. This ardour for storytelling was first aroused by the folk-tales he heard his mother tell him and his sisters especially on moonlit nights, and he believes that this helped him a great deal to become a good storyteller. To his mother too, he says, must be attributed his fair knowledge in the history of the Akan people.

At school, Augustine invariably kept his place at the head of class and showed signs of precocious literary proclivities. Coupled with the stories he heard from his mother, the books he read at school produced a remarkable impression on him so much that he soon decided to write his own stories, the first of which was "Why the Monkey Looks like Man." He never showed these stories to anybody because he thought they were not good enough.

He wrote a poem entitled "Mother Ghana" bemoaning the social and economic woes of his motherland while in school, for which he emerged winner in a sub-regional poetry competition. His introduction to the works of prominent African playwrights such as Efua Sutherland's *Marriage of Anansewa*, Ola Rotimi's *The Gods Are Not To Blame*, and Ama Ata Aidoo's *Anowa* induced him to make his first venture in playwriting. *The King's Wages* is his first play. Augustine is now a professional teacher and pursues a degree in English Language at Valley View University, Ghana.

Characters in the Play

TANO, *an Akan god*

OKOKROKO, *king of an unnamed Akan land*

TUTU, Okokroko's *brother*

BOTA, *Tutu's friend*

OBIYAA, *Tutu's wife*

OHENEWAA, *Tutu and Obiyaa's daughter*

FIRST CHIEF

SECOND CHIEF *members of the King's council,*

THIRD CHIEF *rulers of other towns and villages*

FOURTH CHIEF

THE GHOST

A GUARD

A COOKMAID

A MAID

A PRAISE-SINGER

Townsfolk, Court Attendants, Musicians, etc.

ACT I

The stage is in semidarkness.

A talking drum is heard, bemoaning the wicked absurdities in the heart of man.

In front of us is the palace of the King, a substantial building with two main doors and a thatched roof supported by a row of four wooden pillars. The left door leads to the King's bedchamber and the right door allows a link to the other principal rooms of the house. There are only two windows visible to us, left and right, and they are wholly composed of bamboo slats. On a dais, equidistant from the doors, is the King's throne— an object of exquisite workmanship—with stools grouped about it. Designs of traditional symbols adorn the front wall of the building, and two crossed spears, by way of ornament, hang on either end of the wall. Far on the right, there is a footpath that leads to the homes of the Townsfolk. Along the footpath there is a tree with a massive trunk and tiny branches spreading far into the air. Beyond the outline of the palace a hillock and two coconut trees can be seen, obliterating half of the sky. Far on the left of the palace, there is a boundary of dense flowering shrubs and a household shrine, waist-high and smeared with blood of animals.

Scene 1

When the talking drum stops, the lights come up to depict the brightness of a sunny afternoon. We see **TANO***, an Akan god standing before the palace, clad in dirty tattered clothes and carrying in his hand a walking stick. He takes a few steps forward and begins to speak to us.*

TANO: I am the mighty Tano, he who enfolds the waters and holds the life of man in the hand like an egg. I am the stream that crosses the path; I am the path that the stream crosses. Today I have taken a visible shape and come to the land of my own people, to forewarn their King of what is yet to be and, by so doing, save him from a malice-caused tragedy that approaches his throne.

In the beginning when my father, Odomankoma, had finished His work of creation, He brought down His sacred abode known as the sky, that He would dwell close to these mortal beings called men. So greatly did He love the human race that He disdained not to companion with them, teaching them things beyond mind and matter and vouchsafing all desires of their hearts. But soon pride made its dwelling in their hearts and they began to do what was right in their own eyes. Ergo, righteousness declined and evil became strong. Darkness replaced light, and man, the new creature, proved utterly degenerate. But the last straw that broke the camel's back was an old woman who, on the pretext of pounding fufu, daily struck the Supreme One with a wooden pestle and He, offended by this height of impiety, moved His abode unreachably far up into the celestial regions. Thenceforward, men have had no direct dealings with

Him and the sovereignty of their world has been committed to us gods. To me, Tano, the eldest of the gods, were assigned all the waters and all Akan states beneath the sun. I sit on the waves and my people worship me with sacrifices and oblations. And indeed whoso worships me in truth and humility, them I bless with peace and prosperity.

From time to time, I assume human form and walk among the inhabitants of the earth, offering succour to the good and meting out punishment to the bad. In like manner have I come to this land today, to inform its King of the way in which the future is fated to be accomplished, so as to save him from an evil plot yet to be designed against him by his own flesh and blood. If the King listens to me and does as I will tell him, he shall escape this evil plot and continue to wax greater. But if he listens not and does as seems fit in his own eyes, he shall be cut down like a tree and all that he possesses shall go to his enemy.

(Turns towards the palace.)

Now I see him inside his palace. I must not be known; therefore I shall summon him forth and, to conceal my true identity, tell him I am a blind messenger of the gods.

(Pretending to be blind; shouting)

Where is the King? I seek a moment's audience with the King! I carry a message for him… where is he? A message from the great gods of our land I bring to the King. Where are you, O King? Come forth from your palace that I will give you this message and go back in peace.

(Enter a GUARD from the palace.)

GUARD: What is the reason for this your shouting, my friend?

3

TANO: Who speaks with me?

GUARD: That matters not.

TANO: Oh, my eyes can't see.

GUARD: As if I cared!

TANO: Pray tell me, brother, am I in the royal palace?

GUARD: What do you want here? Answer quickly before my sword severs your head from your body.

TANO: In the name of the gods, do no harm to the poor blind man! I am defenceless— treat me not as you would a foe.

GUARD: I said what do you want here? Answer that and cease provoking me to anger.

TANO: From a far-off village have I come, my brother— climbing hills, crossing streams, and braving the merciless heat of the sun, to deliver a message to the man who wields sovereignty of this land. I humbly beg you, if I'm in his palace, go and bid him come that I may give him the message.

GUARD: What are you saying? You bring a message to the King?

TANO: Yes, my brother.

GUARD: What message?

TANO: A secret word. It is for the King alone and none else has the right to hear it.

GUARD: Well then, go home and come back tomorrow.

TANO: I should go home?

GUARD: You heard me correctly. At the moment the person you seek is having a little doze and must not be disturbed.

TANO *(tolerantly)*: "A little doze"? That's an interesting turn of phrase! Pray go— awaken him for me. Let him know that too much love of the horizontal position is the bane of all good.

GUARD *(scandalized)*: Aha!

TANO: Our elders say he who has not crossed the river cannot insult the crocodile that it has a lump on its snout. Ask the King to chase slumber away from his eyelids, for he isn't free from problems and troubles.

GUARD: Are you as deaf as you are blind, my friend? Or do you want me to borrow a different tongue to speak to you? I said the King is asleep at the moment, so go and come back tomorrow.

TANO: I did hear you, my brother, and I hasten to add that I well know it is generally not considered acceptable for the King to be roused when sleeping. Be that as it may, I cannot go back home until I have given him this message in my mouth. An exigent matter…. So again, I most humbly beg you— go summon him forth for me.

GUARD: Have you, blind man, heard the saying that "If a small bird sings with the voice of a big bird, its voice breaks"?

TANO: Yes, I have.

GUARD: Then off with you!

TANO: And I believe you too have heard that "If a river overflows its bank and passes where it is not known, people there call it a puddle."

GUARD *(affronted)*: What nonsense!

TANO: Much as I wish not to incur your displeasure, brother, I cannot go back home if I don't give my message to the King.

(GUARD draws a sword.)

GUARD: Do you see what I am holding here in my hand, my friend? Oh, I even forgot about your sightlessness! Here— touch it! Do you know what it is? It is a sword. A well-sharpened blade of iron. Now do yourself a favour and wend your way from here before I redden it with your blood.

*(Shouting)*Be off or I will split you into halves! Do you hear what I say? Do you hear what I say?

(Enter CHIEFS *coming into the palace.)*

FIRST CHIEF: What is going on here, our King's servant? From a distance we heard you shouting. What is the matter?

GUARD: My lords, this blind man— He is plaguing me.

SECOND CHIEF: A blind man plaguing you? That provokes mirth, doesn't it? How can a poor blind man plague another man who is blessed with power of sight?

GUARD: He is pestering me, my lords— He seeks an audience of his Majesty.

THIRD CHIEF: True? What for?

GUARD: That I asked him but he is unwilling to tell me.

FOURTH CHIEF: What is it, stranger? Why have you come to the King's palace?

SECOND CHIEF: And why are you "plaguing" the King's servant?

TANO: My eyes cannot see you, brothers; but if I am not quite deceived, the mere tone of your speech tells me you are all good men. Therefore I first greet you.

CHIEFS: Your greetings are well received.

TANO: The object of my coming here is very simple. I am in quest for the King. I have a message for him.

FIRST CHIEF: A message for the King? From whom, if we deserve to know?

TANO: From the gods of our land.

CHIEFS *(surprised)*: The gods?

(They exchange glances.)

THIRD CHIEF: I need hardly say having an audience with his Majesty is always reckoned an honour, isn't it? But, tell me, stranger, am I right in saying that you are a beggar?

TANO: Perhaps you wouldn't have ventured that guess, my brother, if I were a man of dignified appearance. Don't imagine me to be what I'm not because of my clothes.

(CHIEFS look at him doubtfully.)

FIRST CHIEF: Pray tell us this message you bear.

TANO: I am sorry but I seek the royal ear. The message is for the King alone and none else must hear it.

SECOND CHIEF: We cannot know it?

TANO: I am afraid so.

FIRST CHIEF *(meekly)*: Very well then. We have heard you, and we consent. *(To GUARD)* Go at once to his Majesty and tell him that a man is at his door beseeching his immediate presence.

GUARD: I obey my lords.

(Exit GUARD.)

FIRST CHIEF: We ask your pardon, stranger. Pray wait here; the King shall be with you soon.

TANO: Blessings upon your heads, brothers! May the gods who elevate a man so that even his goat becomes elevated elevate you for this deed.

FIRST CHIEF: So may it be, old One. And for going through the fatigue of conveying the King's message, we ask the same for you. *(Good-naturedly)* Now hospitality and good manners incite us to ask you something else. Before the King comes, would you not like to partake of anything?

TANO: No, brothers. Nothing will I feed my belly under the King's roof.

FIRST CHIEF *(mildly surprised)*: And if we may ask, why do you say that?

TANO: Noise and hunting do not go together, my brothers. I am here to deliver a message, not to feast on comestibles.

FOURTH CHIEF *(aside to* **CHIEFS***)*: His clothes may seem filthy but his words are evidence of profound wisdom. I daresay it is true he has a message for the King.

SECOND CHIEF *(Aside to* **FOURTH CHIEF***)*: You seem to echo my own thought. I even say he might be not of this world— you never can tell.

FIRST CHIEF: All right then, stranger. We will not bother you to eat anything here against your will. This is a royal palace, the residence of a most powerful king; anyone who comes here must, as hospitality demands, be welcomed with large-hearted cordiality. But if that person chooses not to eat nor drink anything, it would be quite inhospitable of us to force him or her.

TANO: No need to excuse yourself, brother. I really like your words, though. Politeness shown to unknown guests is a certain source of divine favour. I tender my gratitude.

(Enter **KING OKOKROKO***, followed by* **GUARD***.)*

OKOKROKO: What is it, revered ones? Who is here looking for me?

FIRST CHIEF: This man with a stick, your Majesty.

OKOKROKO: Who is he? And of what land has he declared himself to be a denizen?

FIRST CHIEF: We don't know him, your Majesty, and we haven't questioned him concerning his land and people.

OKOKROKO *(to* **TANO***)*: Welcome to you, friend-stranger. What may your wish be? Is it peace with you?

TANO *(indicating* **CHIEFS***)*: Pray tell me, brothers— am I in the presence of the King?

GUARD *(bellowing)*: None of your insolence, friend! The King asked you a question— answer him!

OKOKROKO: Patience, patience. He is blind— can you not see that? Do be nice. *(To* **TANO***)* What is the cause of your coming to the royal palace, friend-stranger? What do you require of the King?

TANO: King Okokroko, is that you?

OKOKROKO: I indeed.

TANO *(kowtowing)*:

O King Okokroko,

my dear King,

favoured of the gods above all men,

the lion that seizes meat from the paws of other lions,

the mighty porcupine with whom one should never rub bottoms,

he who brings his enemies to their knees,

among all Kings the highest,

may you accept my greeting, mighty one.

May you accept my obeisance.

(He prostrates.)

OKOKROKO *(hugely pleased)*: Hmm! Who is this whose mouth is full of sweetness? Pray stand up that I may see your face. Who are you and from where? Should I address you as my own subject or as a denizen of another land?

TANO: Your most humble subject am I, peerless King. I am a son of this land, born and bred. I bear a secret word to you from the mighty gods of our land. Without food and respite have I come here— half a day's journey away— climbing hills and wading across streams for your sake. Upon my arrival I was told you were wrapped in the arms of a gentle slumber, but I insisted on meeting you so as to give you the message and return home.

OKOKROKO: You have a message for me?

TANO: Even so, your Majesty.

OKOKROKO: Very well then. Let us hear it.

TANO: I am afraid, my Lord, but there are many ears here with us.

OKOKROKO *(confused)*: Many ears?

TANO *(stoutly)*: Firm were the words of the gods: the message I bear shouldn't be told anybody but your Majesty. If you would so have it, my King, bid your servants leave your presence that I make it known to you alone.

OKOKROKO: I see. *(To* **CHIEFS***)* Revered ones—

CHIEFS: Your Majesty.

OKOKROKO: Pray retire to the interior of the palace. I shall soon join you.

CHIEFS: We obey your Majesty.

(Exeunt **CHIEFS** *and* **GUARD.***)*

TANO: Are we now alone, my King?

OKOKROKO: Yes, we are. I am all ears. What message from the gods do you bring me? What do I need to hear alone?

TANO *(gravely)*: I am the bearer of a forewarning to you, my lord King. If you make light of this message and fail to do as I will tell you, your life shall be taken and your name that is now in the mouths of friends and foes alike, shall be wiped from among the inhabitants of the earth. But if you wholeheartedly listen to me and do as I will tell you, you shall surely live and your enemy, whoever he is, shall be put to an open shame.

OKOKROKO *(wryly)*: My enemy?

TANO: If you have no wound, O King, you may think that the housefly is your friend. Don't be deceived about what dwells in the heart of man; for therein dwell many wicked, filthy things. You wield power, my lord King; therefore forget not about your enemies. For if a squirrel dances on a broken branch of a tree, he must not forget about the mouths that are opened underneath him.

OKOKROKO *(with cold politeness)*: I cannot fathom the meaning of your words, my dear guest. Pray speak to your King in plain language.

TANO *(solemnly)*: Be it known to your Majesty that there is a man here in your house who covets your kingly throne and, for it, seeks to end your life. This man is scheming against your life, and to foil his scheme, this is what the gods say I should tell you: you are to drink neither wine nor anything that may make you drunken, the whole of today. For such will be the scheme of your enemy— to kill you with poisoned wine.

OKOKROKO *(not shocked)*: Poisoned wine?

TANO: Yes, your Majesty.

OKOKROKO: And who could that be? Who is my enemy?

TANO: The gods mentioned no name, my King. But if a man takes a lamp to find a snake at night, he must start at his own feet. Be careful of those around you, O King, for man is not a proper object of trust. Everybody is smiling at you, your Majesty, but who can tell what goes on behind their smiling faces?

OKOKROKO *(controlling his uneasiness)*: I do not want to pervert the meaning of your message, my good guest, therefore tell me this and tell me true. Just precisely what do you mean when you say someone "covets your kingly throne and, for it, seeks to end your life"? Do you mean to say that there is a man here in this house who wants to be King and, on that account, has resolved to kill me with poison?

TANO: It is even so, your Majesty. That precisely is what the gods sent me here to tell you.

OKOKROKO *(timidly)*: Oho!

TANO: Are you not surprised to hear that, my King? Isn't that something that curdles your blood? This world is a dark place, O Majesty, so dark that even those of you who are blessed with power of sight have to light your lamps in broad daylight. You have eyes, so you already know whereof I speak. Be on the watch, for man is like the chameleon: because the chameleon changes its colour to match its surrounding, you cannot tell its true colour. Yes, man is like the chicken: because the chicken feeds and wipes its beak on the ground, you cannot tell whether it has fed or not. I am telling you the truth, my King, for I have had sufficient reason to believe what I do believe.

OKOKROKO *(punctiliously)*: Pray have the goodness to tell me something else, my guest.

TANO: I am listening, your Majesty.

OKOKROKO: Did the gods tell you what I have done to offend this person of whom you speak— this my enemy?

TANO: You have done nothing to offend anybody, virtuous King. There's no wrong in your hands. Of a truth, you are not a King who delights in wickedness and thinks evil of his brother-man. Therefore the gods have blessed you beyond measure and made you the greatest among all sovereigns of men. But it is sufficient to say that the enemy of evildoing is an enemy of the evildoer. Keep your eyes open, my King, for the caterpillar that eats the leaf is under the leaf itself. Keep your eyes open, I say again, for your very enemy sits at your table.

OKOKROKO *(nervously analytical)*: Help me know this, my guest, that the doubts of my mind may be dispelled. Indeed you, risking all the untold perils on the road and walking with nobody but a stick as your eye and companion, have done well by conveying this message from the gods to me. May the immortal Ones recompense you for that. But let me ask you this. There is one thing I know, that not to just any mortal man do the gods give a message. So tell me this and tell me true— am I right in thinking that you are a priest?

TANO: No, my lord King, I cannot call myself a priest.

OKOKROKO *(surprised)*: Are you a soothsayer?

TANO: I am no soothsayer, your Majesty.

OKOKROKO: What are you, then? A witch-doctor? A vaticinator? Someone who uses signs to interpret the prognostics of future events?

TANO: Call me a sightless man in dishevelled clothes who happens to be a messenger of the gods.

OKOKROKO *(with ill-concealed vexation)*: Oh, I see! So if you are neither a priest nor a soothsayer nor any of what I said, how do you expect me to believe that it was indeed the gods who sent you?

TANO: I speak the truth and nothing else, my King.

OKOKROKO *(with growing indignation)*: No, my friend, you heard what I said! How do you expect me to believe that your words are true if you are not a priest? What shows that you are a messenger of the gods? Your stick, or your tongue?

TANO: Does my King mean to insinuate that I have wearied his ears with a fabrication?

OKOKROKO: Oh, are you asking me? Yes, that is what I say— and that is the truth. I have seen through you, my friend. Do you think I was born yesterday? Do you think I am a saphead to believe this— what d'you call it— message of yours? You made this tale up that you could find favour in my sight.

TANO *(joylessly)*: Really?

OKOKROKO: You know you are not a priest, but you speak as though you were. Perhaps you do not have the slightest inkling of the consequences of deeds like this. And perhaps you don't know the person you want to try your ruse

13

on. What do you take me for? An empty-headed man? You think I don't know which end is up? And so you pluck a bird in your home and bring it here to ask me what kind of bird it is? No, my friend. You don't teach the paths of the forest to an old gorilla. I am your King— I am blessed with more wisdom than you. *(Calling)* Guard! Guard!

TANO: What is your Majesty doing?

OKOKROKO: He who dances to the music of a madman is himself mad. I can't allow you to be under my roof while you treat the name of the gods irreverently. You speak as truth that which is untrue, and that truly vexes me.

(Enter GUARD.)

GUARD *(bowing)*: What is your Majesty's wish?

OKOKROKO: Get this man instantly out of my palace. He is nothing but a hoodwinker— get him out!

GUARD *(to TANO)*: Come along, my friend. Away with you at once.

TANO: Please permit me to ask the King something.

OKOKROKO: Ask what? *(To GUARD)* Allow him.

TANO: Can my King give me just one reason why he is behaving thus?

OKOKROKO: You ask for one reason, but two will I give you. Firstly, you are polluting the name of the gods. You claim to have been sent by them, but that, of course, is a lie. If it were true that it's the gods who sent you to bring me that so-called message, they wouldn't be so unknowing as not to mention the name of the person by whose hand this evil of which you speak would be done. Need I say, the gods know everything and nothing can we mortal men conceal from their scrutiny. Second reason, you have no respect for me your King. You are a malicious trickster who wouldn't scruple to play his rotten tricks on his own sovereign lord. But do listen, my friend, you can't trick me. No matter how sharp your teeth are, you cannot bite water. Now convey yourself away from my palace and never retrace your steps back.

TANO: I will do that for you, my King. But before I even stir a step, allow me to say one thing to you.

OKOKROKO *(indignantly)*: What?

TANO: Now I know why my lord King professes incredulity at this message I brought him and even seeks to expel me from his palace. You, my King, are doing what you are doing not because the message I brought you sounds far-fetched to you; neither is it because I did anything to injure your feelings. Ah, you dwell inside a forest and yet see no trees! I didn't call myself a priest, nor a soothsayer, nor anything of such a kind, and so you think I am a hoodwinker. What I was supposed to tell you I have already told you. To believe or disbelieve my words is your own choice, my King. But in making your choice, do not forget that if a man refuses to take cheap advice, he ends up buying dear repentance. Do as I was sent to tell you, and you shall live and continue waxing greater. Slight my words, O King, and tragic— yes, extremely tragic— shall your doom be.

OKOKROKO *(severely)*: Guard!

GUARD: Your Majesty.

OKOKROKO: You heard me order you to throw this sightless parrot out of my palace?

GUARD: I did, your Majesty. *(To* **TANO***)* Away with you, my friend! Let's move!

(Exeunt **GUARD** *and* **TANO**. *The talking drum yields death-tones, heard by us alone.* **KING OKOKROKO** *begins to walk about in an agitated way.)*

OKOKROKO *(with abandon)*: What's this? The utterance of the gods? What man is that which just left my house? Who could he be? *(Ruefully)* Of a truth, what he said curdles my blood and chills the marrow in my bones. I don't know if I must trust his words. How can it really be that, having driven him away I am still frightened by those ominous words he uttered? *(**Turns towards the household shrine***)* Is there any truth in his words, gods? Could it be that I have allowed the love I bear my people to blindfold me, making me mistake malignity for goodwill? *(**Resignedly**)* It is only a dead man who has no enemies. Yes, even Kings have enemies. *(**As if something has dawned on him**)* And— why do I even take fright? Why do I let fear seize upon my mind? Are there not in this land numerous priests and soothsayers? How could the gods pass by all of them and speak to a blind man who isn't their servant? *(**With a self-satisfied laugh**)*Ah! That man is a trickster. I was well-nigh deceived by the force of his eloquence. He lied like truth and I had better give no credence to anything he said. *(**Sighing**)*And besides, if a house-gecko is fated to be burnt, what can prevent it from being burnt? Absolutely nothing!

*(Enter **GUARD**.)*

GUARD: Your Majesty, I have sent that trickster away.

OKOKROKO: "That trickster"? Which means you know who he is?

GUARD: I don't, your Majesty. But it scarcely required a second glance to tell me he is a trickster.

OKOKROKO *(stoutly)*: Then I was right. I can tell you, he is a dishonest person.

GUARD: Very right, your Majesty. He is a dishonest person.

OKOKROKO: I don't want to see his face in my palace again, do you hear me?

GUARD: It shall be as the King has ordered.

OKOKROKO *(after sitting on his throne)*: Now go to my brother's house— delay not— and call him for me. Have him come to the palace before the day draws to a close, for I want to send him somewhere.

GUARD: Your brother Tutu?

OKOKROKO: Have I any other beside him?

GUARD: I am sorry, your Majesty.

OKOKROKO: Be quick and do that for me. I shall be inside the palace with the Chiefs.

(He gets up and walks into the palace.)

GUARD: Oh bother! That man Tutu— the very sight of him makes my blood boil. Now I am to go and fetch him. I am going, but with great reluctance. *(Gloomily)* I think it is about time somebody summoned the courage to stop him tickling himself so he can laugh. He thinks he will be king one day, so he has started behaving like one now. He goes about with that his dog, Bota or whatever he calls himself, demanding payment of homage from the people. Oh, that the gods listen to the voice of a nonentity like me! May he never accede to the throne of this land!

(He goes off.)

Scene 2

Enter **TUTU**, *wearing a scowl, and* **BOTA**, *laughing.*

BOTA: Adu Tutu, my master!

TUTU *(irritably)*: What?

BOTA: Adu Tutu, my friend!

TUTU: Speak— my ears are open.

BOTA: Adu Tutu, my brother!

TUTU: I said speak! Or are you deaf?

BOTA: I am not deaf, my master. My ears do work perfectly. Truth told, it merely gladdens my heart to pronounce your name. *(Rhapsodically)* You are my master. Yes, my one and only master. And soon— how soon I cannot tell— you shall be my sovereign Lord and King. You shall be a man of extraordinary power, maker of kings and deposer of kings. Great men will come from afar and near, those who will have heard of your greatness and majesty; they will come to prostrate themselves at your feet and worship the very ground whereon you tread. To you shall belong this land, far and wide as human eye can see. Great towns, luxuriant vegetation, fecund soil, big rivers— you shall gain them all. You shall take many women to wife; you shall beget many offspring, too. You shall have many concubines, and your bed shall never know the coldness of night. What is more: you shall get enormous wealth, treasures of every substance and hue, greater than any other king beneath the sun. Oh, will that not be amazing, my future King? Is that not the desire of your innermost heart?

TUTU: Can't you hold your peace just for a moment, fellow? What profit is there in your incessant chatter?

BOTA: Silence, my future King, is for those sleeping the eternal sleep of death. While I find myself among the living, please permit me to talk.

TUTU: Talk sense then.

(Enter GUARD.)

GUARD: Greetings to my lords.

TUTU *(offhandedly)*: Why are you here?

GUARD: I was on my way to your house, my lord. I am entrusted with a message for you.

TUTU: From whom?

GUARD: From your brother the King. He sends word that you come to the palace straightway.

TUTU *(after a pause)*: Did he say why?

GUARD: He says he would like to send you somewhere.

TUTU: Is that not what he's good at? Go tell him I am coming forthwith.

GUARD: I obey my lord.

(Exit GUARD.)

BOTA: You do surprise me today, my master.

TUTU: And why is that?

BOTA: I don't want to call it "change". But accustomed as I am to seeing you always full of cheerfulness, it beats me why you are in this sullen mood today. My jokes don't provoke laughter. It seems the man I'm speaking to is worlds away from me. *(Laughs in half-suppressed spasms.)* You look like one torn by thoughts. Why, what is ailing my future King?

TUTU *(as if in fear of ridicule)*: It is none of your business, my friend.

BOTA: Ah, listen to that! He is now calling me a bad friend. Isn't that a lie? Ha-ha! Am I not your best friend, the worthiest of your trust, my future King? Have I not known your deepest secrets and shared your worst plights? Come on, unburden yourself to your best friend. What's with this grim face of yours?

19

TUTU *(angrily)*: I said it's none of your business, jolly fellow.

BOTA: You know it is, Tutu.

TUTU: How so?

BOTA: Am I not like a brother to you?

TUTU: Nothing ails me. That does it.

BOTA: Nothing?

TUTU *(angrily)*: Would that not suffice, babbler?

BOTA: No, no, no, my master. Don't act like that. With you have I walked ever since my boyhood days: you are not the kind of person to look so grim about nothing. There is a saying— If the Creator gave the swallow nothing at all, He gave him swiftness in turning. By merely looking at your face, I can easily infer you are afflicted with a mental pain. So don't conceal it and say it. What are the thoughts that make you so ill-humoured today?

TUTU *(sotto voce)*: Oh, can I tell him? This babbler?

BOTA: Adu Tutu—

TUTU *(impatiently)*: What?

BOTA: Don't hesitate to say it.

TUTU: Say what?

BOTA: That which bothers you.

TUTU *(giving in)*: All right, all right, I will tell you. Perhaps that will make you stop being flippant.

BOTA: You don't say.

(A long pause, during which **TUTU** *seems to be cogitating on something. At last, he comes out with it.)*

TUTU: I need your help, Bota. I desperately need your help and well it is that there's nobody here with us.

BOTA *(laughs)*: Now he is talking as a friend, is he not? What help from me do you need?

TUTU: Pray come closer. Walls have ears. Come closer.

BOTA: Closer? Like this?

TUTU: Yes.

BOTA: Now say it.

TUTU *(somberly)*: You are my best friend as you said, Bota, that is why I am going to bare my head to you.

BOTA: I have pricked up my ears.

TUTU *(with cold emphasis)*: All my life I have been a dog to my royal brother and served him with utmost deference. I have loved him like my very own soul and lost no opportunity of promoting his glory among the people. From the rising of the sun to its setting, I till his lands with my hands and fill his barns with food. With good will and lowly-mindedness have I managed his household, and made sure nothing goes wrong. But of all that toil what is my reward? What has the sweat of my toil-worn brow brought me? Nothing. I say, nothing. For thirty-six years, he has been King while I have been a vain expectant of better days. What bitterness have I not gone through? Pain and suffering, which of them have I not endured? While he has been in the lap of luxury, my life has been nothing more than a constant struggle. He thinks only of himself… a thankless man… and doesn't care about me. But no longer can I be his dog while he throws away his bones. And that is why I need your help, Bota. *(With gravity)* I have proposed in my mind to send my brother to an early grave and take possession of all that belongs to him. I want the kingship of this land to be set upon me; I want to see men bow down to me; I want people to address me as "Your Majesty". But, alas, it seems I am after something I am incapable of achieving. Therefore I am burdened with anxious thoughts. So I need your help, Bota. I want you to aid and abet me in getting rid of my brother. You are my most reliable friend, so I expect you not to hesitate to do what I ask of you. Of a surety, my heart can ill afford to rest if I do not accomplish this deed. *(Desperately)* Pray be my accomplice in it, good friend. Be my accomplice and you can be sure of my fervent gratitude when I attain the object at which I have now aimed.

BOTA *(with unceremonious jocularity)*: Adu Tutu…!

TUTU: Bota.

BOTA: Adu Tutu, my future King!

TUTU: I am all ears, my good friend.

BOTA: You need not have spoken as long as that, Adu Tutu. All too well know I those things you said about your brother. It is indeed true that he seeks only his interest and doesn't care about you. Oftentimes have I asked myself if it is true both of you came from the same womb. For I cannot see how a man can by any stretch of the imagination be this wicked to his own brother. I thought maybe he would be good and kind to you since you are his only sibling. But can we blame him? Certainly not. For "It is mine" and "It is ours" are not the same. That's the custom of men, dear friend. When man reaches greatness and all things go well for him, he begins to think for himself alone— no thought in his head for his brother-man. Isn't that the chief cause of our misery today? *(Clears throat.)* Now as regards what you ask of me, Tutu, dispel your fears and set your mind at ease; for I cannot refuse to aid and abet you. There are many paths to the top of a mountain, but the view is always the same. For my part, I bear your brother no ill will; but you are the best of my friends. Together have we walked ever since we were mere boys, twinned as the foreleg and the hind leg of a dog. Therefore if you are enlisting my help to obtain the royal throne, I can't say no to you. I will gladly do all I can to help you effect that purpose.

TUTU: Oh, those are the words of a true friend! Thank you, Bota.

BOTA: Don't thank me, my master. Don't thank me. The Tortoise says, "A hand goes and a hand comes." That is what we are supposed to do as friends— helping each other. I am proffering you my help today. Who knows— I too may need yours tomorrow.

TUTU: Quite true.

BOTA: Don't thank me. *(Aside)* Of course, I am no buffoon; I know it shall soon be his. Is helping him not a guarantee of a royal favour?

TUTU: Well, what do you think…?

BOTA: What do you mean, my future King?

TUTU: How shall we set about it?

BOTA: You mean now?

TUTU: Yes, now. The herbs to apply to a snakebite are quickly plucked. I want to see my brother's dead body before the day passes.

BOTA: Well, before the day passes you will thank me. But, pray, I might have a better idea if you could let me know what is on your mind first.

TUTU *(very solemnly)*: Nothing good is on my mind, dear friend. Nothing but anxious thoughts. You say it… I am agreeable to anything you suggest.

BOTA: No, no, no, Tutu— say something. Wisdom is like a baobab tree, no one person can embrace it.

TUTU: Quite true.

BOTA: Say something. That will be much helpful.

TUTU: All right. If you insist, I will say something. *(With quickened emphasis)* Seeing that the King goes out from the palace every two months to visit his gold mines, I was thinking we could hire some liers and set them in ambush for him when it comes to pass that he goes on such a journey. But in that case, we will have to hire many liers so as to outnumber members of the royal entourage. However, if that idea be not good enough, I was also thinking we could approach one of the King's bodyguards who is apt to barter his loyalty for gold, and engage him to plunge a dagger into the King's bosom tonight.

BOTA *(vehemently)*: No, no, a thousand times no, my future King! If we did either of those, you could be very sure it would be just a matter of time for us to meet our destruction.

TUTU: Give your counsel, then. What ought we to do?

BOTA: What you seek, my master, will be very easy to accomplish if only you will listen to me and do what I will tell you.

TUTU: I am listening.

BOTA: I know of a poison concocted from specially combined admixtures of potent herbs and venom— the best of its kind, if you ask me. This poison induces deep sleep before putting to death. I bought it from a man whose acquaintance I made during one of my trips to the coast. By your leave, we will get it and put it into something that may make drunken— say palm-wine. You shall send that palm-wine to your royal brother when it is time for his repast and make him believe you tapped it yourself. Now listen carefully and keep this well in mind, for we can ill afford any mistake in what we are planning out.

TUTU: My ears are cocked.

BOTA: In your brother's presence, you shall make concealment of yourself, doing nothing to arouse his suspicion. Your evil thought must be clothed with a brotherly act. And with kindly words, you shall lure him to drink the palm-wine, telling him you have already had your fill of it. The poison of which I speak is odourless, therefore it shall be impossible for the King to detect it when drinking the palm-wine. As soon as the palm-wine enters his stomach, he shall begin to feel drowsy and perforce seek his bedchamber. In his sleep, the poison will slowly increase in potency and painlessly drive his soul away from his body—

TUTU *(dryly)*: Whereupon I shall be hanged for regicide, for everybody will certainly get to know that I gave him the palm-wine.

BOTA: By no means, my master. Nobody will get to know that you killed the King. That's the reason why the poison induces deep sleep before it kills. Now if the King in his sleep passes on, people will say he has died a natural death. Is the man not already full of years? Have his limbs not grown weak on account of age? There shall be no reason whatsoever for people to connect you with his death. I say, it shall appear to be the work of fate.

TUTU: Is it as easy as you make it seem?

BOTA: There's nothing to it, my future King, there's nothing to it.

TUTU *(with hopeful emphasis)*: Very well then. I have given ear to you, Bota, and I think I like your plan right well. We shall do all that you have said. But promise me one thing… that you shall breathe no word hereof to any living soul.

BOTA: My lips are sealed, my master, even under threat of decapitation.

TUTU: Very good. Now let us go and get the poison. Thereafter, we shall buy the palm-wine. I know where we will get it fresh.

BOTA: Let's make all haste.

TUTU: Oh, look! This fool is here to bother me again.

(Enter GUARD.)

GUARD: My lord, the King still waits for you inside the palace. Once more, he has bidden me ask you to come there without delay.

TUTU: Well, you can tell the King from me that he should tarry yet a while longer, for I am going to do something on my farm. And tell him that I have realized that his call sounds very urgent, therefore I will be back erelong and come to the palace.

GUARD: But, my lord—

TUTU *(harshly)*: Did I speak with water in my mouth, my friend? Or do you respect the King more than me? I said go and tell him I am going to my farm. *(To* **BOTA***)* Come, my brother, let us make all haste and do what is requisite to be done.

(Exeunt **TUTU** *and* **BOTA***.)*

GUARD *(fiercely contemptuous)*: Oh! Of what is the similitude of this wisdom-lacking man who has no respect for any man under the sun? He is repulsive! Simply repulsive! Look at him… no sign of virtue to show. His likeness is as the likeness of the turkey-cock that puffs up its feathers because it thinks the weather is fair. No, not even the turkey-cock. His likeness is as the likeness of the mistletoe that vies with an orange tree for sunlight. Little does it know what lies in store for it when the fruit-grower comes a-pruning. It baffles me— the nature of men of his ilk. Rankest fools they are— all of them! Why are they full of pride? Why do they vaunt as though they would never see death? They are like smoke: they rise for all eyes to see them, but before long they vanish, leaving behind no good memorial. In the way of evildoing they weary themselves, right up to the time of breathing their last. Ah, vainglorious fools! Alas, one day, through the very doing of their own hands, they shall perish and nobody will remember them.

(He goes off.)

Scene 3

(KING OKOKROKO and CHIEFS sitting in council. Enter GUARD, bows in greeting.)

OKOKROKO: Did I not send you?

GUARD: You did, your Majesty.

OKOKROKO: And where is the man I bade you go and call?

GUARD: He says he is going to do something on his farm, your Majesty.

OKOKROKO: His farm? What is he going to do on his farm?

GUARD: He could not say precisely, your Majesty.

OKOKROKO *(after a pause)*: Very well. You are at liberty to retire. But make sure you call him for me when you see him again.

GUARD: I obey your Majesty.

(Exit GUARD.)

OKOKROKO: I want you, brothers, to tell me something.

CHIEFS: We are listening, your Majesty.

OKOKROKO: It is— something that weighs so heavily upon my thoughtful mind. A question, and I want an answer from you. I know I am your sovereign lord, and by virtue of that, you accord me great respect over all men. But pray do nowise out of that respect say what is not true so as to please me. Let your answer, I pray you, conform with reality and be free of deceit.

FIRST CHIEF: To your Majesty we dare not speak falsely.

OKOKROKO: Tell me this…. How do you see me as King?

CHIEFS *(at sea)*: How do we see your Majesty as King?

27

OKOKROKO: Yes— In the fulfilment of my duties, I mean. Am I good King, ruling with wisdom, courage, and high sense of duty? Or am I bad King, evil, tyrannical, and self-seeking? Pray speak as your heart bids you.

(A pause ensues.)

FIRST CHIEF: Your Majesty…

OKOKROKO: I am all ears, old one.

FIRST CHIEF: Of a truth, the likeness of words is as the likeness of arrows: once they escape the barriers of a man's mouth, they can never go back. For that reason, men must exercise circumspection so as not to peril their lives when addressing Kings. So it is— when a man talks and talks and talks, he causes his own ruination by unruly speech. Nonetheless, I cannot call something white if it be black. I will not mince matters because I revere you as my sovereign lord; I'll say the truth because it is what I hold as a principle. *(Significantly)* I am a man full of years and have had the honour of serving five kings including you, my lord King; yet have I not seen a leader like you. Your equal, it is true, is difficult to find among rulers. When a king has plenty of milk, his people drink of him. Because you rule us with a good heart, we are blessed with supreme joy and contentment. We flourish like foliage, and our enemies live in extreme dread of us. Who has not heard of your wisdom as sovereign of the land? Who does not know of your sublimity as King? It has been spread abroad through all men's mouths. It is even the subject of conversation when our womenfolk meet at the marketplaces. Indeed you are the paradigm of the good king and to the gods we all are very grateful to have you ruling over us.

SECOND CHIEF: What he says, your Majesty, is true. You are the mighty elephant that we follow therefore we cannot get wet by the dew on the bushes. Under you, our kingdom has expanded phenomenally and our people have nothing to grumble at. Peace is abroad in our land and the gods have never forsaken us in all that we do. All these signify that you are a good person, and we are proud of you as our supreme lord.

OKOKROKO *(aside)*: Indeed, these people bear me no malice. That blind man— did I not say it was deceit he wanted to practise upon me? *(Aloud)* I believe what you have said, my brothers. And I thank you very much for telling me the truth. I often say that people around us are like the surface of water: we look at them to see our own reflection. And a man mustn't judge his appearance by the number of people who look at him, but by the number of people who smile at him.

CHIEFS: Very true!

OKOKROKO: I do believe what you told me, not because of the universal veneration shown to me as King, but rather because of the apparent ease and gladness I see in the lives of my people. In all my days as King of the land, I have learnt something that is of vital importance. What is it? I have learnt that in the unrestricted exercise of royal power, a king is like someone holding in the palm of their hand an egg: if they hold the egg too firmly, it will drip through their fingers; and if they hold it too loosely, it will fall on the ground and break. Therefore I have made it the underlying principle of my life to put the interest of others before mine— Yes, but not so as a weakling, but as a man of granite and of considerable mental energy.*(Meditatively)* I don't want to do to any man what I would him not do to me. None is perfect under the sun, my brothers. However, if we exercised a close scrutiny over our deeds, there would be nothing like enmity among us.

CHIEFS: Your words are true, your Majesty.

OKOKROKO: That is what I think, revered ones. Had all men loved one another, our world would have been a peaceful one, unfamiliar with pain and trouble.

CHIEFS: Yes, your Majesty!

(Enter TUTU, carrying a pot of palm-wine.)

TUTU: My greetings to your Majesty.

OKOKROKO: Greetings, dear brother.

TUTU *(to CHIEFS):* My greetings to our Chiefs.

CHIEFS: Your greetings are well received, Tutu.

OKOKROKO: Where are you coming from, brother? I have been looking for you.

TUTU: That is true, your Majesty. But pardon me for making tarrying— I had to go quickly and check something on my farm.

OKOKROKO: So said the guard. I purposed sending you somewhere, but... *(looking skywards)*...it seems the day has well-nigh ended, and I have decided to postpone it till tomorrow.

TUTU: True? I am very sorry I couldn't come as early as your Majesty wanted.

OKOKROKO: No need to apologize. I believe what you went to do is equally important.

(CHIEFS stand up.)

FIRST CHIEF: Your Majesty...

OKOKROKO: Brothers—

FIRST CHIEF: We beg leave to go home.

OKOKROKO: Oh, so soon? Your company makes time pass agreeably. *(With charm)* Very well. Go you in peace. And don't forget to convey my compliments to your families. The gods be with you.

CHIEFS: And be with your Majesty.

(KING OKOKROKO stands up and walks them to the footpath. They exit. Throughout the ensuing

conversation, **TUTU**'s *actions are characterized by fidgetiness.)*

TUTU *(a slightly shaky voice)*: I had to go and check my palm trees. Have I made it known to your Majesty that I have started tapping palm-wine?

OKOKROKO *(surprised)*: Palm wine? No, you haven't. Not as a bread-winning job, I believe? When did you start?

TUTU: Just last week.

OKOKROKO *(gladly)*: And how is it going?

TUTU: Too early to tell, your Majesty, but I am optimistic. I have more than fifty palm trees to fell. *(Aside)* Why is my voice tremulous? Oh, he will see through my plan!

OKOKROKO: You are doing the right thing, brother. And it gives me joy to see you doing something profitable with your time. Henceforward, let me know anytime you are going to the farm; I will ask my slaves to go with you.

TUT: Much obliged, your Majesty. *(Pause.)* But I am not so sure if I am a good tapper. You see, there are many tappers in this town and I just started it. I don't know if, as they put it, I have good hands. I remember you were once a tapper yourself before your accession to the throne. Doubtless you have expert knowledge in tapping and I can rely on your judgment. *(Trying to steady his voice)*You see this pot here? I have filled it with palm-wine, the one I just collected this afternoon when I went to the farm. I know you have a fondness for fresh palm-wine, so I brought this for your repast. Now pray taste it and tell me if you think I have good hands.

OKOKROKO: Oh, really? Will that be necessary?

TUTU *(with a qualm)*: Not so, not so, your Majesty. I merely wanted to know if I am not wasting my time as a tapper. But I will not bother you if you care not to oblige me.

OKOKROKO *(smiling)*: Care not to oblige you? What a thing to say! You well know I would gladly do whatever you ask of me. Put the pot down here and fetch me a calabash from my bedchamber. I will taste it and tell you what I think.

TUTU: I'm grateful, your Majesty.

*(***TUTU*** *goes into the palace while* **KING OKOKROKO** *walks to his throne and sits down. A few moments later,* **TUTU** *re-enters with a calabash.)*

OKOKROKO: Here.

TUTU: Permit me, your Majesty, to do the honours.

OKOKROKO: You have my leave.

*(***TUTU*** *lifts the pot, gives it a stirring-up, and fills the calabash for the King.)*

TUTU *(desperately)*: Now taste it— taste it and see.

OKOKROKO: Certainly not, brother. Libation first. He who drinks without pouring a few drops on the ground is an ingrate to the gods.

TUTU: How right!

*(***KING OKOKROKO*** *removes his sandals, steps on them, and bares his chest as a sign of reverence to the gods.)*

OKOKROKO: Odomankoma, giver of rain and sunshine,

> we cannot give You a drink; but we can show You it:
> So, here is it.
> Mother Earth, our birth-giver, as for you we can give a drink.
> So, we ask you to come and drink.
> Numerous gods and goddesses of our land,
> we beseech you to grant us your presence.
> Spirits of our forebears and familiar spirits around us,
> we invite you, too, to come and partake of this drink.
> When we call one, we call all:

a dog does not forget where it is thrown food.
You give us peace, you give us joy,
you made us who we are today.
We therefore pour this palm-wine to express our gratitude
to you for your blessings.
Today your son Tutu has started tapping palm-wine.
Bless this work of his hand and prosper him.
We also ask you to bless all our men with wealth;
and bless our women with housefuls of children.
May the day never dawn when evil shall betide us.
If any man wishes evil for us, let him die accursed,
and let us attend his funeral with a horrible dance.
Drink— drink— drink!

(He empties the calabash on the ground.)

TUTU *(his voice still tremulous)*: You need a refill, your Majesty.

(He refills the calabash.)

OKOKROKO: I like its look.

TUTU *(aside)*: Oh, I am now in great fear of detection!

(OKOKROKO takes a mouthful of the palm-wine, savours it and nods.)

OKOKROKO: And I like its taste too. It is very sweet— sweet and quaffable.

TUTU *(voice becoming more tremulous)*: I am mighty glad to hear that, your Majesty. *(Aside)* Why is my voice still trembling?

(OKOKROKO continues to drink.)

OKOKROKO: You have done very nice work. Anyone who tastes it will think you have tapped palm wine for years. Very good hands. But…will you not join me?

TUTU: Oh, no, your Majesty. I have already had my fill.

OKOKROKO: Is that so? Then sit by me and let's talk. You have done well. *(Dolefully)*I wish I could tap like you.

TUTU: But you were a good tapper, your Majesty. Weren't you?

OKOKROKO: Yes, yes, I was. But I am talking about the physical strength to do it. Now it is not as when I was young. I wish I could tap like you today. Old age is a troublesome guest, brother.

TUTU: That's true.

OKOKROKO: Now I am a fragile man. My knees have grown weary and my constitution will not do half of the things I want it to do. I cannot weed, I cannot farm, I cannot even go to the bush to fetch herbs as I used to. Nothing do I do. It is a pity— human beings. We are like this palm-wine I am drinking. When young, we are sweet— very delightful. In old age, we lose our sweetness and become sour, virtually good for nothing.

(He drinks.)

TUTU: It is such a pity.

OKOKROKO: Indeed. Then consider the brevity of man's life— the frailty of this mortal body. We pass away like a breeze; our days are all as an arrow shot in the air. Just yesterday I was a toddler; today I am a hoary-headed man; tomorrow he whom they call Death will come knocking my door— time to bid the world adieu.

TUTU *(guilty)*: Death? You are not going to die soon, your Majesty.

OKOKROKO: You think so? *(Laughs grimly.)* And who are we to tell death when to come for us?

TUTU: Well, I feel not at liberty to argue about the matter. But— look at you. You have more days ahead of you.

OKOKROKO: The ladder of death is there for everyone to climb, dear brother. The dry leaf falls, the green leaf falls. Need I say, he is no respecter of persons. We cannot tell him whom to take and when to take. And if you ask me, the earlier he comes for us, the better for all of us.

TUTU: Why is that?

OKOKROKO: Look at the grave, Tutu. Is it not a humbling phenomenon? It reminds you of why we ought to love one another, does it not?

TUTU *(aside)*: Now he is talking about love and the grave. Perfectly understandable, isn't it?

*(***OKOKROKO** *drinks.)*

OKOKROKO: Love is what we need in this cold world, brother. There is no medicine to cure hatred. Come to think of it— If you love your brother, will you harbour any desire to do him an ill?

TUTU: No, you will not.

OKOKROKO: Will you allow covetousness to dwell in your heart, your eyes after his property?

TUTU *(trying not to appear tormented)*: No, you will not.

OKOKROKO: Will you recompense him with evil for all the good he did you, not stopping your hand even if your heart isn't in harmony with your body?

TUTU *(aside)*: I am beginning to fear this talk he is talking.

(Sepulchral silence.)

OKOKROKO: Many a time, I sit down in long spells of brooding, searching for answers to some questions about this wearisome life. Sometimes I even see some things and become disposed to sit upon the ground and, like a child, give way to my tears. I cannot, though meditating much, understand them. Without controversy they are matters beyond human comprehension. Diseases, disasters, decadence, death— We toil and toil and toil, and eventually lose all that we toil for because of death. Why? Why is death among us?

TUTU *(sententiously)*: As you said, such things are beyond our power of fathoming. Only the immortal Ones understand them.

OKOKROKO: Indeed, only they do. *(He yawns.)*

TUTU *(aside)*: Is he yawning? *(Aloud)* You look tired, your Majesty.

OKOKROKO *(ignoring him)*: Completely baffling it is— man's life. From waking to sleeping we weary ourselves amassing wealth. Very soon, we are gone and all our suffering comes to naught. *(Dully)* Love is what we need.

TUTU *(fear in his voice)*: Love is what we need.

OKOKROKO: About seventy years ago, there was a man called Kaakaaku who lived in this town. In those days I was hardly more than a child, standing as high as a man's waist, and you, needless to say, had not been born then. Kaakaaku was a man of great substance, wealthier than any other man among all the people in this land. He possessed many sheep, many goats, many farms, and many slaves. But the problem with him was that, he also possessed a foolish heart. He was wicked, deficient in wisdom, avaricious, and exceedingly proud. It never occurred to Kaakaaku that he, like us, was a mortal man. And so, his greatest joy lived in extortion and oppression of others. *(Drinks.)* Thus he lived till one day something terrible happened to him. *(Chuckles grimly.)* One day he was struck with a shameful malady, such a one as sends men to their early graves. All his wealth and his friends forsook him, and day and night alike he wailed, seeking the sweet deliverance of death. But death, his new enemy, refused to grant his wish. And Kaakaaku lay on his sickbed for fifteen agonizing years, his body rotting and discharging some bad-smelling fluid. He could not eat, he could not drink, he could not sleep. He became a burden for the whole town and almost every citizen was summoned to proffer their opinion as to what should be done concerning him. Some said we should banish him from the land; some also said we should allow him to rot in his house; while there were also that said we should send him to the most powerful medicine-men in the world. But in the end, after doing all they could and without his regaining health, his kinsmen had no option but to bury him while there still was breath in his nostrils.

TUTU *(in some surprise)*: What? They buried him alive?

OKOKROKO: Yes, they buried him alive. *(Yawns.)* And some people said that even after his burial, they could still hear him from his grave beseeching death to come and take him. I do recall that his story was used by us children in a song; so that beside his own name, he received the posthumous nickname "Death's Enemy". *(Laughs eerily.)* That is how the Creator created His world, Tutu. If a man gives bad food to his own stomach, it drums for him to dance.

(He yawns again.)

TUTU: Pray say no more, your Majesty. All your actions betoken bodily fatigue.

OKOKROKO: Yes, and I do not know why. My eyelids have suddenly become heavy with sleep.

TUTU: Why not seek your bedchamber? I think it would do you a world of good.

OKOKROKO: You are right. I must go get some sleep.

TUTU: To bed with your Majesty. The body soon becomes weak.

OKOKROKO: You can say that again, brother. The body soon becomes weak.

TUTU: Get you to your bedchamber, your Majesty.

OKOKROKO: I will see you when I wake up.

(KING OKOROKO totters to his feet and, with difficulty, walks into the palace.)

TUTU *(with a sigh of relief)*: Now there's a pleasant ache in my heart and I don't know if I should call it joy or an evil against myself. One thing I know, that joy never comes unsought. But if it comes, it does so with an evil against oneself. Now what so long has hovered just beyond my reach is about to be mine. *(Forces a laugh.)* Very soon Okokroko shall find himself in his grave and I, Tutu, the stone that wears down the axe, will find myself on the throne of this land. Mine shall be the kingdom and all therein.

Away with you, hungriness!
Away with you, days of overmuch desires!
Where is the gloom that hid my name
among the sons and daughters of men?
With gentle silent steps greatness comes,
with soft-sandaled feet it wends its way hitherwards.
Anguish and pain that keep me company,
my heart's overpowering longings,
the self-pity that among my tears has its dwelling—
all, be prepared to go away!
Come forth, days of dazzling glory.
Come forth, days of unparalleled mightiness.
Do help me remove this cloak of obscurity,
these threadbare habiliments of life I am wearing.

(He goes off. The talking drum is heard, lamenting the madness in covetousness.)

Scene 4

(CHIEFS enter, towards the palace.)

FIRST CHIEF: Is it not just a few moments ago that we all left here, brothers? Then who among us called us back?

SECOND CHIEF: It is I, brother.

FIRST CHIEF: Why this meeting?

SECOND CHIEF: I bring you serious tidings.

FIRST CHIEF: Serious tidings?

SECOND CHIEF: We have to be very careful, brothers, otherwise it may well be that before this month passes, the Awisa people will swoop down upon us.

THIRD CHIEF: The Awisa people?

FIRST CHIEF: What makes you say that?

SECOND CHIEF: A man just returned from Kurusi that is close to Awisa, and he bears tidings that their king has made a pact with all the chiefs along the coast to engage in a struggle to liberate the lands under his Majesty's control. According to him, the king is trying to arouse the chiefs to a new way of thinking, saying his Majesty our King has been a wicked Over-lord who for more than three decades now has developed his own kingdom and neglected the lands he conquered in war. The king of Awisa has therefore persuaded them to be united under his power and to disobey and reject his Majesty as their Over-lord. And not only that— he has also begun distributing enormous sums of money among the chiefs, who in general seemed to have fallen for his wiles. Now he has sworn an oath that before this month ends, he shall drink his wine from his Majesty's skull.

(The others are scandalized by the news.)

FOURTH CHIEF: This is ludicrous. Somebody is playing with the tail of a lion!

THIRD CHIEF: That man is looking for the annihilation of his people, I say!

SECOND CHIEF: He must be taught a lesson, brothers. He must be made to rue his decision!

FIRST CHIEF: Patience, patience, gentlemen. Pray stay your anger. As the boy looks around for a stone to throw at the bird, the bird also looks around for a place to flee to. It is true that our enemies have made their decision to attack us. But what do we do in that case? We also lay our heads together to see how best we can defend ourselves against them, right?

SECOND CHIEF: That is right!

FIRST CHIEF: We all know that by comparison with our kingdom, Awisa is but a village. That is not to say that we need to be complacent. By no means! What we need to do is to whet our swords and put on our war-smocks. If the enemy comes, we unite our strong arms and destroy his hosts. That's what we must do as men of valour. Indeed, our tribe is not a tribe of women and wild ducks. Our tribe is a tribe of dauntless, warlike men; men who do not shudder at the sight of blood. So, if it is war the Awisa people are asking for, it is war we shall give them. But first, our King must be apprised of the situation, for he is the owner of the land.

SECOND CHIEF: Well-spoken!

FOURTH CHIEF (*portentously*): The king of Awisa is a very shrewd man, brothers. Let us beware.

THIRD CHIEF: If he is shrewd, my brother, we will show him we are shrewder.

FIRST CHIEF: Time is tight— let us bear the tidings to his Majesty. Where are the court attendants? They must go summon the King for us.

SECOND CHIEF: A young lady is coming this way.

FIRST CHIEF: Oh, good!

(Enter one of the King's cook maids, crying.)
COOKMAID: *Buei! Buei! Buei!*

> *Asem aba o!*
> *Asem aba o!*
> *Asem aba o!*

FIRST CHIEF: Why are you bawling your eyes out, young woman? What has befallen you?

SECOND CHIEF: What is the matter, my daughter? Tell us if haply we may know.

COOKMAID: *Asem aba o!*

> *Asem aba o!*
> *Asem aba o!*

THIRD CHIEF: From your wailing we deduce that a mishap has befallen you, but you do yourself no good by refusing to tell us what it is and why it is. Pray cease your grief and tell us so that we can help you. Does the eye too not suffer when the nose is hurt?

COOKMAID: O, our dear Chiefs…

CHIEFS: Yes?

COOKMAID: Esteemed lords of our kingdom—

FOURTH CHIEF: Waste no time mentioning appellations, young woman. Why are you doing this? Are we not men and you a woman? Have we not seen more terrible things in war and in hunting? Control your emotions and tell us what the problem is.

COOKMAID: I don't know how to say it, my lords. What I have seen with my eyes is beyond my tongue to tell.

FOURTH CHIEF: What have you seen? Tell it like it is.

COOKMAID: King Okokroko, our Chiefs—

CHIEFS: Yes? What has the King done?

COOKMAID *(impulsively)*: He is dead!

CHIEFS: What?

41

COOKMAID: King Okokroko is dead— oh, dead and gone!

CHIEFS: Where?

COOKMAID: In his bedchamber.

(CHIEFS rush into the King's bedchamber. Meanwhile, the Townsfolk begin to come in from all directions, inquiring in whispers about what has happened.)

FIRST MAN: I heard the sound of wailing.

SECOND MAN: So did I.

FIRST WOMAN: What has happened?

SECOND WOMAN: Your guess is as good as mine, my sister.

THIRD WOMAN: Look— that woman there is in tears.

THIRD MAN: Is the King dead?

FIRST WOMAN

SECOND WOMAN   Thunder will strike your mouth!

THIRD WOMAN

THIRD MAN: What is my offence, my sisters? Is the King not a mortal being like us?

FIRST WOMAN: Oh, shut your filthy mouth, my friend! The King is a mortal being like your father!

THIRD MAN: Now keep a civil tongue in your head, woman, or you will see that I too am uncouth.

FIRST MAN: Hush, hush! Let's not fight. The Chiefs are coming. Let's hear from them what has happened.

(Enter CHIEFS.)

FIRST WOMAN: Pray have the goodness to tell us, our dear Chiefs. What has happened in the palace?

FIRST CHIEF: Oh, monstrous, our people! I cannot believe my eyes.

SECOND CHIEF: I am overwhelmed with astonishment, our dear sons and daughters. Horror has tied my tongue.

THIRD CHIEF: My heart grows cold with grief.

FIRST WOMAN: What has happened, revered ones? Pray tell us if we deserve to know.

FIRST CHIEF: Lament, people; for a mighty tree has fallen.

TOWNSPEOPLE *(shocked)***:** What?

FOURTH CHIEF: A mighty tree has fallen. The man you loved dearly is no more!

THIRD MAN: Oh, I said it! *(To women)*Now whose mouth will thunder strike? Tell me. Whose mouth?

(The women begin to mourn. The talking drum is heard, telling of the King's death.)

FIRST WOMAN *(mourning)***:** O death! O death! Whom will you let be?

SECOND WOMAN: Our strength is gone! Alas for us! Our strength is gone! We are all as good as dead. What shall become of our land?

THIRD WOMAN: O King Okokroko, our dear King! We will forever miss you.

FIRST CHIEF: Pray curb your emotions, my daughters. It is too early to shed tears for the man. Remember he was not just a king, but the greatest of Kings. Therefore let us all keep dry eyes for now. We shall have many days to mourn him.

(Enter TUTU.)

TUTU: What is going on here, Chiefs? I heard the sound of the talking drum from afar. What is it in aid of?

FIRST CHIEF: All is not well, son. All is not well.

TUTU: What do you mean by that? What has happened in the palace?

FIRST CHIEF: You go to your brother's bedchamber; what you ask and has not been answered shall you see for yourself.

(TUTU runs into the King's bedchamber.)

SECOND CHIEF: I still don't understand. How could a man who was just conversing with us be snatched away like that?

FOURTH CHIEF: I don't understand it either.

(A silence.)

FIRST CHIEF: I daresay we are wrong about one thing, brothers.

SECOND CHIEF: And that is to say…?

FIRST CHIEF *(trying to speak in a whisper)*: It's about the manner of the King's death. I do not think he died a natural death.

CHIEFS *(aghast)*: What?

(Murmurs of surprise among the Townsfolk.)

SECOND CHIEF: What talk, brother! You do not think the King died a natural death?

FIRST CHIEF: Yes.

FOURTH CHIEF: Then, pray tell us: Of what did he die? Did you see him in a pool of blood with a dagger buried in his breast? Or did you see his neck twisted?

FIRST CHIEF *(advisedly)*: I think— I think the King was poisoned.

CHIEFS *(staggered)*: Poisoned?

FIRST CHIEF: Yes, my brothers. Trust me, I know a lot about poisoning and there is no doubt about what I say. Did you not see for yourselves how pale his skin had become? And the foam at his mouth, did you not see it too?

(Enter TUTU, crying.)

TUTU: O gods of our land, from where comes this? What deed did we do to merit this from you, immortal Ones?

Is it something we ought to have done but never bothered to do? Or is it a wrongful conduct of our ancestors in the past? Why have you snatched this staff out of our hands, gods? Why have you cut off this piece of cord that holds the broom together? Pray tell us our offence. Pray help us unravel the mystery of our wrongdoing.

SECOND CHIEF: Show yourself a man, son— a man weeps not. It is the Supreme Being who has broken our leg, and it is He who will teach us how to limp.

TUTU: I cannot possibly understand why my brother has been snatched away so unexpectedly. Oh, why does he go this way? Just a few moments ago I was with him, and he looked quite healthy and strong.

A WOMAN AMONG THE CROWD: May the gods never rest till they bring a worse fate on his murderer.

(Abruptly, **TUTU** *stops crying.)*

TUTU: "Murderer"? Did you say "murderer"? Who told you my brother was murdered?

THE WOMAN *(indicating* **FIRST CHIEF***)*: He did. He says he does not think the King died a natural death.

TUTU *(to* **FIRST CHIEF***)*: What? Is that true?

FIRST CHIEF: I never said your brother was murdered, my son. Pray do not misrepresent what I said. What I meant was that, I am apt to believe— and I choose my words advisedly—I am apt to believe that your brother the King did not die of a natural cause.

TUTU: In other words, he took his own life?

FIRST CHIEF: Not so, not so. Your brother, I daresay, died of poisoning.

TUTU *(caught)*: Poisoning? What talk is this? How do you know he died of poisoning?

FIRST CHIEF: The signs on him show it, my son.

TUTU: What signs?

FIRST CHIEF: I think you saw them yourself— the colour of stains on his cheeks and his discoloured lips. And the pallor of his skin, did you not see it? And the foam and vomit around his mouth? They are all signs of poisoning. I even checked his orifices and saw some fluid. When I smelt around his mouth, I realized that just before his death he drank palm-wine.

THIRD CHIEF *(shocked)*: Palm-wine?

FIRST CHIEF: Yes. But I don't know if that was the cause of his death.

TUTU *(aside)*: Oh, I must do something, lest I become the silliest murderer on earth! Bota was wrong: the poison has betrayed signs. They will get to know it and hang me for killing the King! I must do something! *(Aloud to* **FIRST CHIEF***)*So you say you think my brother died of poisoning, huh? Who was the first person to see him dead?

SECOND CHIEF: One of his own cook maids.

TUTU: Where is she?

SECOND CHIEF: There.

TUTU: Oh, good. Pray tell her to draw close.

SECOND CHIEF: Draw close, my daughter. The King's brother wishes to have a word with you.

*(*COOKMAID *obeys.)*

TUTU: I beg you, young woman, look at me and answer what I ask you. Is it true that you were the first person to see my brother dead in his bedchamber today?

COOKMAID: Yes, it is true, my lord. For two years now have I been of service to his Majesty, preparing his meals and arranging his dining table. Today I went to his bedchamber to inform him that his lunch had been served when I saw that he had passed into the deep sleep of death.

TUTU: Very good. And is there any truth in it too that he was neither strangled nor stabbed, but, as I have been made to believe, killed with poison? Pray answer.

COOKMAID *(lachrymosely)*: I do not know, my lord, if he—

TUTU *(severely)*: Will you stop shedding those tears and answer my question! Was my brother killed with poison?

COOKMAID *(wiping her tears)*: I do not know if he was killed with poison, my lord.

TUTU: Oho! You do not know? A ridiculous answer! You are one of the King's cook maids, are you not? And you are telling me you do not know if he was killed with poison? That is untruly said, my dear. You are speaking with a forked tongue. Say something else.

COOKMAID: I am telling you the truth, my lord.

TUTU: No, you are not.

COOKMAID: I cannot lie to you, my lord.

TUTU: Yes, you can.

COOKMAID *(tears flowing)*: Oh, I swear I cannot.

TUTU: Oh, I swear you can.

THIRD CHIEF: Tutu…

TUTU *(tetchily)*: What?

THIRD CHIEF: I do not think what you are doing is giving us help. Let not this young woman be the one to answer those questions you have with regards to the King's death. According to her, she merely saw his body when she went to his bedchamber… and not that it mattered. Whether he died of poisoning or not, if you ask me, she is not the right person to make that known to us.

TUTU: Just hold your tongue, old man! Otherwise, I unleash my temper on you. And who appointed you her advocate? You are advanced in years, therefore I expect you to say something sensible or, better still, refrain from speech if you think there's no wisdom in that head of yours. *(To* **COOKMAID***)* Now I await an answer to my question. Was my brother killed with poison?

COOKMAID: I do not know, my lord.

TUTU: Maybe I have to rephrase my question, for clearly I can see that you do not understand me well. You have said it yourself, have you not, that you were the first person in this whole palace to see my brother's dead body. And the Chiefs here are saying that, from some physical signs on the body, they infer he was killed with poison. The information I am seeking— all that I am asking for— is, do you think, as do the Chiefs, that my brother was killed with poison? Cease shedding those false tears and speak! I need a forthright answer.

*(*COOKMAID *rubs her tears.)*

COOKMAID: Well, my lord—

TUTU: Yes?

COOKMAID: If—

TUTU: If what?

COOKMAID: If that is their inference, I cannot in anywise contradict them.

TUTU: Very good! That precisely is what I wanted to hear from you. A very good answer. Now here is your next question— let your answer be as good and in accord with truthfulness. For whatever your fate shall be today, shall depend on the answer you shall give. *(Indicating* **CHIEFS***)* Do you see these greybeards here? Which one of them sent you to poison my brother?

CHIEFS *(thunderstruck)*: Ehn? What was that?

SECOND CHIEF: Have you taken leave of your senses, Tutu?

TUTU: Oh, wait but a little and you all shall know for yourselves. *(To* **COOKMAID***)* You are trying my patience, young woman. I pray, do not waste my time. Point out with the finger to me the one who sent you to poison my brother.

COOKMAID *(in tears)*: I do not know what you are talking about, my lord.

TUTU: Oh, you do not know! Then do not worry. A tree that does not know how to dance is taught by the wind. You will perforce be talking differently once I decide what to do with you.

COOKMAID: By the gods, my lord, I know nothing about the King's death… Oh, nothing! And what good would it do me to commit such evil?

TUTU: For the sake of gold dust, the fetish priest swallows an arrow. We all know what money is capable of making human beings do nowadays.

COOKMAID: That is true, but—

TUTU: Nothing can you say to throw dust in my eyes, young woman. You are a malicious liar and I will make you rue the day you ever accepted to poison my brother.

COOKMAID: I did not poison the King, my lord. I did not. I know nothing about what you are accusing me of. You can inquire into the matter. If you find out that I am lying, you can have me executed by the cruellest death you know.

TUTU: Be patient, my dear. You will certainly get that— all in good time.

(Voices from the crowd:)

FIRST VOICE: Death to the King's cook maid! She is a murderess!

SECOND VOICE: What has she done?

THIRD VOICE: She is innocent! Leave her be!

FOURTH VOICE: She conspired with others to kill the King. Make her drain her own cup of evil to its very dregs!

A WOMAN: My daughter, if you know anything of the King's death, pray hesitate not to say it.

TUTU: Oh, let her be mute if she so chooses. The eye that looks at the sun will not need an adviser before it blinks. Where are the executioners? Will somebody go and fetch me the executioners?

COOKMAID *(kneeling)*: I beg you, O my lord. I kneel at your feet to seek preservation of my life.

TUTU: Where are the executioners?

THIRD CHIEF *(aside to* **CHIEFS***)*: What is he doing?

SECOND CHIEF: He wants to put her to death!

THIRD CHIEF: No, no, no, that is not the advisable course of action. We must not allow him to do that. Let us counsel him to stop it; the cook maid may be innocent.

FIRST CHIEF: Tutu—

TUTU *(unheeding; to* **GUARD***)*: You there, go quickly and fetch me the executioners, will you?

GUARD: I obey my lord.

(Exit **GUARD***.)*

COOKMAID: Be merciful to me, my lord; I entreat you for my life. Pray do not have me put to death on account of something of which I am guiltless.

TUTU: I am going to hand you over to the executioners, young woman, and they will make you suffer a ghastly fate. If you go to the realm of the dead and come back, you will learn how to tell the truth.

FIRST CHIEF: I pray you, Tutu, listen to me—

TUTU *(harshly)*: What again?

FIRST CHIEF: I know you are filled with great anger at the moment, and I say, right excusable is your feeling. But now stay your anger and deign to listen to my advice, lest you take an action and have regrets for it afterwards.

TUTU: Say what you want to say.

FIRST CHIEF: It is true that you loved your brother, but there is no gainsaying we did the same.

TUTU *(trying sarcasm)*: Oh, is that not obvious?

FIRST CHIEF: It is true he came from the same womb as you, but do not forget he was our sovereign Lord and King. And as our King, we venerated him, served him, and obeyed him more than any other man under the sun. Therefore if grief has come upon you by reason of his untimely death, do know grief has come upon us too. Not in anywise am I counselling you to cease from seeking out facts that led to his death. But if you do not mind my saying so, what you are doing now seems headlong and impetuous. There is an old adage that if a man has patience, he can cut up an ant and see its entrails. What is the meaning of that? It means that if a man has patience, there is nothing under the sun he cannot do. The cook maid here has told us what happened and has forsworn any knowledge of his Majesty's death. It is true that she was the first person to see him dead, but from that mere fact we cannot conclude that she has a hand in his poisoning. I pray you therefore to forgo this your hot feeling. I would have thought it would be part of wisdom for us to give the matter some time. Let us— you and the council of Chiefs here— meet after here and inquire into the matter thoroughly, taking one thing with another. That is the duty of the council of Chiefs. Please do not harden your heart and resent what I tell you. Just as good medicine may taste bitter to the tongue, even so good advice may sound foolish to the ear. But if you will readily lay my counsel to heart and do as I have told you, nothing covered will remain covered. For truth is like oil in water: it always comes to the surface for all eyes to see it. I cease speaking.

(TUTU forces a scornful laugh.)

51

TUTU: It grieves me very much, people of our land, to see men who think they are blessed with wisdom merely because they are given to incessant talk, and yet when they talk their mouths pour out words not far from foolishness. Yes, wisdom is like the noses in our faces: every man carries his own. However, if the men whom we regard as repository of knowledge open their mouths and we hear nothing but asininity and silliness, then sore is my soul to say that we have a very long way to go. *(To* **FIRST CHIEF***)* That was an idle speech, old man. You ought not to have spoken like that. In future, anytime you are in public, make sure you think before opening your mouth to speak; for that is what wise men do. They think before they speak. And if you suppose you are good at dishing out advice, you go to the bush and advise the partridge. Advise the partridge to leave the bush and come home because the chicken is his brother.

CHIEFS *(scandalized)*: What nonsense was that? What is with this young man today?

FIRST CHIEF: It is abundantly clear, Tutu, that you do not know what you are doing; therefore I shall let your insult go unanswered. You can ignore my advice and put this young woman to death on an unsubstantiated charge. But if you do so, you must not forget that her blood shall be laid upon you and you shall be tormented for the rest of your days. And mark well my words: it may delay in coming. But if you do not carry it on black hair, you shall surely carry it on grey hair.

TUTU: Your words hold no terrors for me, old man. Let happen to me whatever may happen; I am ready for it.

(Enter **GUARD** *and executioners.)*

GUARD: The executioners are here, my lord.

TUTU: Oh, good, good! Come closer, my men. Come and take this murderess away. It is better for her to die than to live. Take her away… let her neck feel the edge of the sword. She killed my brother; she too must die.

(As they seize her, the lights go down.)

(CURTAIN)

ACT II

The stage is exactly as it was in the beginning of the First Act. At the rise of the curtain, we see every part of it in complete darkness and hear the talking drum announcing the commencement of the Second Act.

Scene 1

A spotlight comes down and reveals **TANO** *who is now clad in clothes of a priest and holds in his hand an iron staff tufted with eagle's feathers. He smiles knowingly at us, waits for the talking drum to subside, and then takes a few steps forward to address us.*

TANO: Thirty days have gone by since I, Tano,
the foremost among the race of the gods,
came to this land of my people to forewarn their king
of what was fated to be.
Thus did I to save the King from an evil plot
designed against him by his own brother.
But a self-willed man that he was, he slighted my word
and thrust me out of his palace, calling me a hoodwinker.
Now, alas, Okokroko has joined his ancestors in death
and his kingdom has been given to his very murderer.
But thirty days after his death, his soul cries to us
elder gods for vengeance upon the man who killed him.
Of a truth, murder is a heinous act and whoso commits it
shall never go unpunished.
Therefore today I, Tano, as the central guardian of this land,
have changed my form from god to man

and come here in the guise and likeness of one of my own priests,

to mete out condign punishment to Tutu

for his wrongdoing and make sure his brother's spirit is propitiated.

But not so fast—I shall tell Tutu what is requisite to be done

to escape the foresaid punishment,

only to ensure that he comes to destruction in the very end.

(He goes off. The drum in the background stops playing.)

Scene 2
(TWO CITIZENS enter along the footpath.)

FIRST CITIZEN: Say, brother— is there any truth in it that our new King is making a feast in his royal palace today?

SECOND CITIZEN: What are you? A stranger?

FIRST CITIZEN: Profoundly deaf, maybe.

SECOND CITIZEN: The town crier has announced this thing for more than a week now.

FIRST CITIZEN: Oho! And how come I never heard of it?

SECOND CITIZEN: I think we need to get a remedy for your deafness.

FIRST CITIZEN: I even thought it was not true when it was told me.

SECOND CITIZEN: It is true, my brother. The King is giving a big feast in his palace today. And everybody is invited.

FIRST CITIZEN: That much I heard, and I couldn't bring myself to understand why he is doing so. Is it to flaunt his wealth or to show us his benevolence?

SECOND CITIZEN: You sound like someone asking why the firefly produces light.

FIRST CITIZEN: My ears had not so much as caught anything of it until this morning when, after I had chanced upon two of my kinsmen, one of them asked me whether I was going to the feast. I asked him what feast, and he said the King's feast. In fact, I was struck with surprise when he told me everything about it.

SECOND CITIZEN: No matter how you slice it, my brother, what the King is doing is completely unseemly. To give a feast barely a fortnight after your brother's funeral, is like spitting on his very corpse. I wonder why he cannot bide

57

his time and why nobody is even telling him to stop what he is doing.

FIRST CITIZEN: I think we must lay the whole blame on our Chiefs. Is it not their responsibility to hold the man in check? They, all of a sudden, seem to have become as children in his hands.

SECOND CITIZEN: You may well say that, my brother. They are weak, for one thing. But can we blame them? Tell me, brother, as you live: where have you ever seen or heard a chief rise against his own king? Tell me, have you ever seen or heard that before? Of course not. For that will be like forfeiting his very chieftaincy.

FIRST CITIZEN: Acquiescence!

SECOND CITIZEN: That's the thin end of the wedge. And besides, our new King himself is not a man to be counselled.

FIRST CITIZEN: You are quite right. Very like him. I always say it—Tutu is nothing like his late brother. He is wholly devoid of the excellent qualities every true leader ought to possess.

SECOND CITIZEN: Is there not a good reason why the chicken cannot sound like the pigeon? The chicken is a chicken, the pigeon a pigeon. Now look— our streets are thronged with boisterous men and women, disorderly. They are all heading towards the palace for the feast. Sacrifices, I hear, have been sent to all the shrines in the land and the gods have given the King the go-ahead.

FIRST CITIZEN: But it seems not everybody is ready for the King's feast. Look at this fellow coming.

(Enter a **DRUNKARD**, *clad in black and singing a dirge.)*

DRUNKARD: We sing the song of our saddened hearts,
　　We sing the song of our past heroes,

We sing the song we know so well.
What death has done no-one can tell.
The fetish dance is gone, mere turning remains;
Memory comes back to us with tears and pains.
Mother Eagle now sleeps, the eaglets become prey.
How danger looms with each new return of day!
Our household hearths have become so cold,
None to give us warmth: we miss days of old.
A piece of wood is stuck between our teeth;
True it is, a cloven stone cannot be stitched.
With many a sigh, we look at that yawning grave
Which have swallowed our men mighty and brave.
These silent ones who lie lower than the sands—
They too have wielded power in their hands.
We sing the song of our saddened hearts,
We sing the song of our past heroes,
We sing the song we know so well,
What death has done no-one can tell.

SECOND CITIZEN: Greetings to you, my dear brother. Pray tell us, why do you sing this song on such a day?

DRUNKARD: Oh, the sorrow that preys on my mind is beyond assuagement!

SECOND CITIZEN: Sorrow?

DRUNKARD: Yes, today is a day of sorrow. With decent grief I mourn our late king Okokroko. I mourn that dread lion who made our kingdom what it is.

SECOND CITIZEN: Is that so? Then I am a bit surprised.

DRUNKARD: Surprised?

SECOND CITIZEN: Time has flown, my brother. Thirty days have come and gone since the old King journeyed to the world of our ancestors. And you well know we all came out, lamented him becomingly, and gave him a burial of honour as befits a great king. And so this thing you do, in my opinion, isn't right. How long will you give yourself to wine on a pretext of mourning a man who has already been mourned?

DRUNKARD *(feigning anger)*: This is an affront, my friend! I am offended by your words.

SECOND CITIZEN: Why do you take it wrongly, my brother? No, it is rather what you are doing that is an affront. It is a sad affront not only to the old King you profess to mourn, but also to his younger brother who now sits on our royal throne.

DRUNKARD: I have nothing to do with his younger brother, my friend. And why do you bandy these words with me?

SECOND CITIZEN: To be sure, you do ill to be mourning someone on such a day as this. Don't you know, or at least, haven't you heard from the town-crier, that our new King is giving a feast in his palace today?

DRUNKARD: Oho! It is only a goat tired of living that goes to the feast of a lion.

SECOND CITIZEN: What do you mean by that?

DRUNKARD: I mean it is only a fool to whom proverbs must be explained after they are said.

SECOND CITIZEN *(hurt)*: Perhaps the wine you have been quaffing has mounted your head and made you oblivious of words coming out of your mouth. That notwithstanding, I shall reply you in like manner, lest you take me for a man deficient in wit.*(Ditto)* It is only a fool who, when he sees a swollen leg, says it is fatness.

DRUNKARD *(mockingly)*: Oh, good. Now you have shown your foolish wisdom. I trust you will seldom speak anyhow henceforward.

SECOND CITIZEN: Your drunkenness may be an excuse, my friend, but he who wants to be respected must first respect himself.

DRUNKARD: Well-taken, brother, well-taken. Now permit me to continue my mourning:

> We sing the song of our saddened hearts.
> We sing the song of our past heroes.
> We sing the song we know so well.
> What death has done no-one can tell.
> Indeed, death is a scar that never heals,
> A thief who cares not what he steals,
> The habiliments everybody will one day don:
> Son will bury father, father will bury son.
> Okokroko was our King, a King like no other;
> Our master-lord he was, a friend and a father;
> He was the great elephant we followed every day,
> So never got we entangled with creepers in our way.
> Alas! Where has our King and warrior gone,
> This warrior who many a fierce battle won?
> O death, what is this you have done to us?
> Why have you sundered our souls thus?

SECOND CITIZEN *(to* **FIRST CITIZEN***)*: Oh, look. Here comes the King's wife. Let us greet her and go our way, for this man here is stoking up my anger.

(Enter **OBIYAA** *and* **OHENEWAA**, *followed by two Maids from the palace.)*

CITIZENS: Greetings to the virtuous wife of the King.

OBIYAA: Greetings to you, my dear brothers. I do trust you are all getting prepared for the feast?

CITIZENS: Yes, we are, our lady.

DRUNKARD *(falsely)*: The feast? What feast?

OBIYAA: The King's feast, my brother.

DRUNKARD: Nothing have I heard of the King's feast.

OBIYAA: True? Then know it from me: the King is holding a large feast in the royal palace today and everybody is invited, including you. You do know that this is the first time since his Majesty's accession to the throne that such a ceremony is taking place. Therefore not only will it be an occasion of great merriment and rejoicing, but also a suitable opportunity for him the King to express his gratitude to the good people of this land. For he is extremely grateful to you for the love and loyalty you showed him during both his coronation and his brother's funeral. And so all of you are invited to come and be partakers of this feast.

DRUNKARD *(sardonically)*: Oh, now I understand! Even if a goat becomes a sheep, there will always be dark spots on its skin.

OBIYAA *(confused)*: And that is to say?

DRUNKARD: Some things are better left unsaid, your highness.

FIRST CITIZEN: The King has done well in this, our lady.

SECOND CITIZEN: Quite so, our lady.

OBIYAA: Both of you will come, I make no doubt?

CITIZENS: It will be remiss of us not to, our lady.

OBIYAA *(to* **DRUNKARD***)*: What about you, my brother? Will you come?

DRUNKARD: I? Don't worry about me, our King's wife. A ghost doesn't wait for the living to eat before it joins them. I have already begun my feast here.

OBIYAA: But your clothes— are you mourning or feasting?

DRUNKARD *(belches)*: Both, both. You see, the life of our society is a life in which exuberance and somberness alternate. Sometimes we mourn, sometimes we make merry.

The teeth that laugh are also those that bite. Not long ago we were in mourning, singing dirges and wearing black to betoken our grief. But today your husband says he is going to make a big feast in his glorious palace. That shows the chameleons we all are. And so do our heads: sometimes we allow them to work, sometimes we hold them in abeyance. Our likeness is as the likeness of small children who cannot tell the dissimilarity between a monkey and a chimpanzee. Alas, alas, alas! We are a people heading towards a bottomless deep, blindfolded by the blackness of our ignorance. We forget heroes that merit heroes' honour, and instead give that honour to spineless, deedless braggarts. *(Belches.)*Oh, people say that I drink like a palm-weevil, but I think alcohol is a bringer of reason. It turns my mind to wisdom and helps me shun ways of reasonless men.

OBIYAA: Save your words, brother. I asked you a simple question: will you come to the King's feast?

DRUNKARD: I will not praise the rat-trap because I want to eat rat, your highness.

SECOND CITIZEN *(irked)*: Why listen to him, our lady? People of his ilk don't deserve your attention.

DRUNKARD: Oh, so you are insulting me, eh? You shall presently see who have a fouler mouth, you or I.

OBIYAA: Enough, enough— no more of this! This is no time for insolent language, I pray. The King has a dim view of that kind of behaviour and will be very annoyed to see you do this. Today is a great day, so cease trading insults. Go you home, gentlemen, and you, my brother, go you also. The feast will begin very soon, and I would like to see all of you in this palace.

FIRST CITIZEN: We will go, our lady; but before that, may we most respectfully ask you to convey our well wishes to the King for us.

OBIYAA: I will, with the greatest pleasure. The gods be with you.

CITIZENS: And with your highness.

(The two **CITIZENS** *go off.)*

DRUNKARD *(ditto)*: When you go, our King's wife, tell your husband that,

*(singing)*We sing the song of our saddened hearts,

We sing the song of our past heroes, etc.

(He goes off, wobbling.)

OBIYAA: Come, come, maidens. Bend down your ears and listen to what I tell you. This is a royal feast, therefore I want no disgrace. It hardly need be said that it is our duty to dispense hospitality to our guests according to the etiquette of the palace. Now I am asking the two of you to take charge of everything that has to do with this ceremony. That is not to say that I am asking you to behave as though you were the matriarchs of the house. If you encounter any problem, make it known to me first. And if you need anything, draw my attention to it as soon as you can. Do you hear me?

MAIDS: Yes, our lady.

OBIYAA: Very good. Now tell me, are you done cooking that palm-nut soup?

MAIDS: Yes, our lady.

OBIYAA: Which means, all is at the ready for the feast?

MAIDS: Yes, our lady.

OHENEWAA: What about wine, mother? Where will we get wine for the guests?

OBIYAA: I do not think that should be our headache, my dear. It is a job for the men. But your father did assure me there would be plenty of it during the feast. Come on now, Ohenewaa. I can see the townsfolk coming. Let us get inside and put on something formal.

(Exeunt.)

Scene 3
*(**TOWNSFOLK** enter, singing and dancing.)*

FIRST TOWNSMAN: Truth be told, brothers, our new King is worthy of praise in that he has invited every one of us to this feast. I don't know what to say; I am as glad as though my wife had presented me with twins.

SECOND TOWNSMAN: You speak truly, my dear brother. What the King has done clearly bespeaks his love for all. He is king for the rich as well as for the poor. I call him the big-breast-that-feeds-countless-mouths. A good king, he!

THIRD TOWNSMAN: We have complete confidence in his unselfishness as ruler of the land. This kingdom will continue to be great under his reign.

FOURTH TOWNSMAN: Our King is wise!

FIFTH TOWNSMAN: Not half!

FIRST TOWNSMAN: Let us sing a song while waiting for him.

(They burst into a song.)
Song:
Yen hene ye kessie
Yen hene ye obrempon
Nhyira na yeresre ama no
Nana brebre, wotirinkwa daa!
(They dance around the stage.)

SECOND TOWNSMAN: Those who are best praised in this world are the ones whose own works have already praised them. Our elders even say it in a proverb: The man who is honoured, has first honoured himself.

THIRD TOWNSMAN *(with emphasis)*: Our new King has first honoured himself, so we ought to honour him all the more.

FOURTH TOWNSMAN: As long as the gods are gods, may his throne remain.

FIFTH TOWNSMAN: May the crown weigh light on his head.

SECOND TOWNSMAN: And may his bed never know coldness of the night.

(They sing and dance again.)

> **Song:**
>
> *Anigyie aba oo.*
>
> *Ahoto aba.*
>
> *Osee! Yema wo amo!*
>
> *Asomdwoei aba oo,*
>
> *Adepa aba.*
>
> *Osee! Yema wo amo!*

(Enter a **COURT-CRIER.***)*

COURT-CRIER: Pray silence for his Majesty the King!

(Singing and dancing stop abruptly.)

SECOND TOWNSMAN: What! The King is coming.

THIRD TOWNSMAN *(childishly)*: The King is coming? Where is he? I want to see him!

FOURTH TOWNSMAN: Now you will be quiet, fellow. You are making noise.

(Quiet is restored. Horns and drums.)

COURT-CRIER: Lo, he is coming!

> The mighty one is coming!
>
> The lion among men is coming!
>
> Let all stand up and make him obeisance.
>
> With homage let all reverence the person of

the King.

(All the **TOWNSFOLK** *stand up. Enter a procession of* **TUTU, OBIYAA, OHENEWAA** *and the King's retinue of Chiefs and bodyguards. Bringing up the rear*

is **BOTA,** *together with other members of the King's household. A* **PRAISE-SINGER** *addresses* **TUTU.***)*

PRAISE-SINGER: Homage to you, dread lion!

Homage to you, slayer of pythons.

It is true that no dew ever competed with the sun.

Yes, it is true that

no king ever competed with you, King Tutu.

If a boy says he wants to tie water with a string,

I ask him if he means the water in the pot

or the water in the river. In the same way,

if a man says he can defeat you our King,

I ask him if he means in his dream or in reality.

Never compare a fly with an elephant;

never compare a king with our King.

For our King is the mightiest of Kings:

yes, a King like no other.

As a giant tree stands in the heart of a forest,

even so stands he in the heart of our land,

sheltering us shivering birds with his sturdy boughs

and giving eatables to the ones enfeebled with hunger.

(Voices from the crowd:)

FIRST VOICE: We love you, our King!

SECOND VOICE: May your kingship last long!

*(***CHIEFS** *motion crowd to keep quiet.)*

PRAISE-SINGER: When the lion roars in the forest,

all animals become quiet.

Let all be quiet for the lion among men,

for he is about to speak.

(Turns to the King.)

Now silence reigns in your palace, mighty one;
you have possession of every ear.

Your children yearn to hear words of your
mouth.

Speak to them.

Speak to them.

Speak to them.

(He withdraws.)

TUTU: Good citizens of our land, on behalf of the royal household, I hail you all a great welcome to my palace. To say that I am glad today, will be but expressing my feelings less than they actually are; for the joy in my heart is so overwhelming that it wells my eyes with tears, and I cannot employ sufficient words to describe it. In solemn truth, my people, we are obligated to render thanks to the gods at all times. Now I am King, but it is none of my doing. For a piece of iron can only become what the blacksmith says it should become. It is the gods who have made me King; it is they that have cast an eye of benevolence upon me. And not me alone, but every citizen of this land. And so, as we make merry today, it remains for us to call that to mind and let there be thankfulness. To you too, my people, I am bound to express my heartfelt gratitude— even so, to express my gratitude with unceasing breath. If a forest shelters you, you do not call it a jungle. Through unanimous manifestations of loyalty and commitment to my glorious throne, you have made me a thankful man. And I must say that it does my heart good today to see all of us gathered here as children of one and the same womb. It is an excellent reminder of what unity can do; for it is by the strength of their number, that ants are able to carry a grasshopper from a field to their nest. Let us, therefore, continue to love one another and, with a greater sense of togetherness, live in all peace and harmony. Notwithstanding all that, my people, I also speak with a sorrowing heart. In truth, I consider what we are doing here as eating a sweet fruit that has a bitter aftertaste. For I can hardly hold back my tears when I call to remembrance the great tragedy that befell this land not long ago. Thirty days have gone by now since my brother, King Okokroko, met his tragic and untimely death.

(Enter **GHOST** *of King Okokroko, invisible to all but* **TUTU**.*)*

His life which he dedicated to serving his people so well was taken by the wicked hand of his own cook maid. We all know the kind of leader he was— so selfless and wise. Yes, he was the proverbial hen who knew what her chicks would eat and never failed to peck it down. He loved everybody and never all his life did he wrong his fellow man.

GHOST *(eerily)*: Then why? Why did you kill me?

TUTU: Who are you? And what is that you said?

FIRST TOWNSMAN: Is my Lord talking to me?

TUTU: No, not you. I am talking to that man beside you.

SECOND TOWNSMAN: My name is Ofosu, your Majesty. I am from the house of—

TUTU: Not you, not you. I am speaking to that old man there. The old man in white. And, oh, by the gods! His face, his height, his bearing— all are like those of my late brother. Elder brother, is that you?

GHOST: It is time for you to be like me. I have come for you! I have come for you!

TUTU *(screaming)*: What! A ghost! A ghost! He is a ghost! Somebody help me! Somebody help— he is a ghost!

CHIEFS: Who is a ghost?

TUTU: There, there… the man in white. He is a ghost! O, help me! He is coming.

CHIEFS: Who exactly?

TUTU: That old man. Are you people blind? The old man in white… Somebody help me!

CHIEFS: We do not see him.

TUTU: For goodness' sake, you do not see him because he is a ghost! Do not let him take me… He says it is time for me to be like him. He is coming for me… O, please help me! The man is a ghost and he is advancing towards me!

CHIEFS: What do we do now?

TUTU: Help me! Help me!

CHIEFS: Let us take him inside.

(CHIEFS huddle round TUTU and accompany him into the palace. OBIYAA and OHENEWAA follow them; GHOST disappears.)

FIRST TOWNSMAN: What just happened?

SECOND TOWNSMAN: In fact, it was on the tip of my tongue to say "The King has gone mad."

FIRST TOWNSMAN: Oh, what a shame!

THIRD TOWNSMAN: Did you see what he was doing? *(Mimicking)* "A ghost! A ghost! He is a ghost!"

FOURTH TOWNSMAN: This is something unheard-of. A King going mad!

BOTA: Pray do not say that, fellow-citizens. The King is not going mad. Do be patient. He will soon be back and the feast will continue.

FIRST TOWNSMAN: Listen to this man. Does he think we are children?

SECOND TOWNSMAN: We will exercise no patience, my friend. We saw the man with our own eyes. He is going mad.

THIRD TOWNSMAN: Come, people. Let us go away from this place. We cannot feast in the house of a madman.

ALL: Yes, let us go.

(Exeunt TOWNSFOLK.*)*

BOTA: O gods, what is happening? What is happening to my friend? Is he going mad? No. By no means! If he goes mad right now, then all my services to him will have been fruitless. That cannot be. The knot tied by a wise man cannot be untied by a fool. I must do something. Oh, I must. All these years of our friendship, all these efforts of mine to endear myself to him, cannot be in vain.

(He goes off.)

Scene 4

(A few moments later. CHIEFS come out of the palace and begin to talk about what has happened.)

SECOND CHIEF: I wonder what that really was.

THIRD CHIEF: Likewise, brother. Why did he behave that way? In front of all these people! Madness or what?

FOURTH CHIEF: I think he was merely seeing things.

SECOND CHIEF: Madness... seeing things... are they not the same?

THIRD CHIEF: Something is wrong somewhere, brothers. No-one knows what the elephant ate to make himself so big. Only the King knows what is haunting him.

FOURTH CHIEF: I think you are right. He has, I venture to say, done something to which we are not privy. Let us ask him to tell us the real truth. For if nothing touches the palm fronds, they do not rustle.

FIRST CHIEF: And why should this thing be a matter of wonder to you, brothers? What one of you can tell me that this thing which is now happening was never anticipated?

SECOND CHIEF: What can you mean by that?

FIRST CHIEF: It ought to have sufficed to conclude that what is happening would happen when we have already seen Tutu act so wrongfully and foolishly. Have you all forgotten what he did on the day his brother died? How he precipitated in action and had that poor maiden beheaded without examination of the truth? You see, he threw the caution to the winds when I told him her blood would be laid upon his head. *(Chuckles.)* The goat thought it was dirtying its owner's wall, not knowing it was tearing off its own skin.

THIRD CHIEF: If I understand you well, Tutu is now being punished as a result of putting that innocent girl to death?

FIRST CHIEF: Such is what life has taught me, brothers. He who brings home a carcass should expect to battle with flies. Tutu derided my advice and acted in the grip of emotions, little did he know what would follow. Now you see the peril of anger, what it has done to him. Anger is like a wanderer: it doesn't live in one man's house. But when it comes to yours, you must not give it a seat. *(Demurely)* It saddens me, brothers, and turns my heart cold with terror when I think of what fate has in store for this land, ruled by a King like ours.

SECOND CHIEF: I perceive in your words something akin to ill will. Why do you talk like that?

FIRST CHIEF: I am not afraid to say it, my brother. If your child is dancing horribly, do not ask him to dance as he pleases; rather be frank and tell him his dance is horrible. I certainly bear Tutu no ill will. However, I fear that, with him on the throne, this kingdom is doomed to fall. At every turn, I see signs portending nothing but evil; I dread the future of our land. As day is entirely different from night, even so is Tutu entirely different from his late brother. He is self-centred, imprudent, and doesn't have a humble bone in his body. Look at him. He is now King, but he knows nothing about the art of ruling.

FOURTH CHIEF: You are right, my brother. Tutu is just an abecedarian when it comes to our royal custom. I always say that to my wives.

SECOND CHIEF: Watch your mouths, my brothers. I need hardly remind you that the man of whom you speak is our King. Even if the elephant is thin, he is still the lord of the jungle.

THIRD CHIEF: Hush, hush! I see his wife coming. *(Enter OBIYAA.)*

SECOND CHIEF: Our King's wife, pray tell us: how fares the King now?

OBIYAA: He is as well as anybody, my lord. He is now reposing in his bedchamber. But he vehemently prohibits all inquiries respecting the cause of his unusual behaviour today, and that is why I have come back here.

SECOND CHIEF: In truth, our King's wife, we cannot account for the King's strange behaviour. What happened is even difficult for us to understand.

OBIYAA *(dismally)*: Now I don't know whether I'm coming or going. Never in time past has he done anything like it.

THIRD CHIEF: Don't concern yourself, our lady. I believe your husband shall soon do well.

OBIYAA: Thanks for your words, my lord.

THIRD CHIEF: For now, he must get a short rest. When he wakes up, forget not something must be given him to eat.

OBIYAA: I will see to that.

FOURTH CHIEF: Look; here comes Bota, and out of breath. Where did he go after what happened?

(Enter BOTA.)

OBIYAA: Where have you been, Bota? I thought I would see you near your friend in times like this.

BOTA: I implore your forgiveness, my lady, if it seemed I was nowhere to be found after what happened in the palace. For immediately after the incident, I ran as quickly as my legs could carry me to summon the Priest of Tano, if perhaps he could come and tell us the cause of the King's unusual behaviour. He has accepted to come and will be here erelong.

OBIYAA: That's very thoughtful of you, Bota. Your loyalty and support to my husband shall never be forgotten.

BOTA: And how fares he now, my lady?

OBIYAA: Much better, much better. He has stopped screaming and is now in his bedchamber. However, he is reticent about what's wrong with him, for which reason I am much worried.

FIRST CHIEF: Our King's wife, now we must go home. We shall certainly come back at nightfall to see how the King is doing.

OBIYAA: Be it so, revered ones. Well and truly thankful are we for what you have already done. May the gods requite you with every blessing for us.

CHIEFS: So may it be, our King's wife.

(Exeunt CHIEFS.)

OBIYAA: Let me ask you a question, Bota.

BOTA: Do, my lady.

OBIYAA: Of the ordinary course of events, you are the King's chief friend and constant companion. You, I daresay, know him even better than I his wife do. And he confides in no-one but you. Therefore tell me this and tell me true. Has he in words or in deed, purposed or purposeless, within the palace or without it, offended any man such to warrant what happened to him today?

BOTA: Certainly not, my lady. Certainly not. Your husband is nothing like that. He is a man who treads warily and always makes sure not to step on the feet of others.

OBIYAA: If that is so, why did what happened today happen? You saw him screaming in the presence of the whole town that a ghost was coming for him, didn't you? What do you think is the matter with him? Why did you even afterwards go to summon the Priest of Tano? Is there anything I should know?

BOTA *(conspiratorially)*: I think, my lady, that an ill-designing person is using sorcery against your husband.

OBIYAA: Sorcery? What talk! Why would anybody want to do that?

BOTA: As a matter of fact, my lady, your husband's kingship has thrust many noses out of joint and put jealousy in many bosoms. I cannot say who, but I am inclined to think it was by one of those men who just left here, that this odious sorcery was practised today. You saw how they were secretly delighted when he was screaming? I tell you it was the Chiefs.

OBIYAA: The Chiefs? You mean his own Chiefs used sorcery against him? What word is this, Bota? But you said yourself that the King walks warily. If that is true, I cannot see why somebody would want to use sorcery against him.

BOTA: It does not necessarily take you to offend somebody before they become your enemy, my lady. Dance on a rock and he who wants to be your enemy will accuse you of splashing water on him.

OBIYAA: What you are saying is true, but I still think there is something I should know. *(The palace door opens.)* I see my husband coming. I will leave now, but pray inquire of him the truth of the matter. I will talk to you later.

(Enter TUTU. OBIYAA curtsies and goes back into the palace.)

BOTA: Mighty lord of mine, it is said that if you see a hunter coming back from hunting with nothing but mushrooms, then you must not ask him how his day was. However, I cannot, even as I see you looking so crestfallen and disturbingly quiet, help asking you the question everybody in this palace wants to ask you. Pray tell me, my King, what ails you? What made you do what you did today in the presence of all the people?

TUTU *(dully)*: I was not feeling well— that is all.

BOTA: I mean not this to be an insult, my King, but I think you are not telling me the truth. Go outside this palace and listen to what the people are saying because of what happened here. "The King has gone mad" goes from mouth to mouth. They are spoiling your name, great one. Pray say it, what is the matter? Was anybody using sorcery against you?

TUTU: What sorcery?

BOTA: Then what, my King?

TUTU: I would rather not talk about it. Perhaps it is enough to say that I wasn't feeling well.

(*BOTA bursts into laughter.*)

BOTA: You have no idea how funny you sounded when you said that, my King.

TUTU (*losing his temper*): Funny? What is funny about what I said? What makes you say that, eh? Oh, I see! Continue laughing, dear fellow. Rejoice at my hurt. You are not to blame, are you? I know you feel nothing for my suffering. How can the crab suffer from headache when it has no head? It is not your fault that you take pleasure in my plight. Blinded by envy, I murdered my own brother— a godless act against my own flesh and blood. Now his ghost is coming after me and I am screaming for help, is that not funny?

BOTA (*stops the laughter abruptly*): Your brother's ghost?

TUTU: Are you asking me? You are a glad spectator of my suffering… so continue laughing.

BOTA: I pray your pardon, my King. I acted in a most silly way. But what you are telling me— is it true?

TUTU: Never mind, good friend. My suffering is none of your concern.

BOTA: I am very sorry, my King. I never meant to make mockery of your suffering. It is like… that never entered my head.

TUTU: Really? Then tell me what entered your head. What did you think? That I was going mad, right? Well, now I am mad. Profoundly mad.

BOTA: You must understand me rightly, my King. I am in great perplexity about this. How come you saw your brother's ghost and I didn't? Did I not aid and abet you in sending him to his grave?

TUTU: Yes, you did. But has he come to torment you? No, he has not. Maybe it is not always true that the accomplice is as bad as the thief.

BOTA: It still beats me.

TUTU: And I wonder why that is. Did you kill the man? You didn't. It was I who poisoned him, and he is after me, not you. When the lizard eats pepper, why should the frog be the one to feel its hotness?

(A pause ensues.)

BOTA: And your wife—

TUTU *(briskly)*: Talk not about my wife!

BOTA: Why?

TUTU: That woman has suffered enough on my account. I want no more troubles added upon those I have already put her through.

BOTA: So what do tell I her?

TUTU *(reflectively)*: Just let her know nothing is wrong with me.

BOTA: If only that will suffice!

TUTU: Will stop bothersome questioning, at least.

(Pause.)

BOTA: I have summoned the Priest of Tano to come and see you. Perhaps he can tell you what needs to be done.

TUTU: And you did that without so much as a by-your-leave?

BOTA: Pardon me, my King, but I did not know what else to do. I thought he could be of help.

TUTU: And what help can I expect from that man? You know I hate him. He was a very good friend of my brother's, and I have decided to have nothing to do with him.

BOTA: I know.

(Pause.)

TUTU: So, did he accept to come?

BOTA: Yes, he did.

TUTU: I am all astonishment!

BOTA: He will be here any moment from now.

TUTU *(sotto voce)***:** He must hurry his steps then.

(Enter GUARD.)

GUARD: Your Majesty, the Priest of Tano is here to see you.

TUTU: Oh, he is here already! Go and bid him in.

GUARD: I obey your Majesty.

(Exit GUARD.)

BOTA: With flattering words, my King, let us enlist his aid. He would do whatever you ask of him.

TUTU: That man is many things, Bota, and you know being a soft touch isn't one of them.

BOTA: He is a man, my King. To be sure, he has the capacity to share the distress and anguish of others.

TUTU: I don't know what to tell him. I'm like a child now. *(Helplessly)*Come on, tell me something. It is you who went to call him. What do you think I must tell him? Should I tell the whole truth? No need to cover it with subtlety?

BOTA: Truth is a hard morsel, my King, but it causes no constipation. Tell him the naked truth, no colouring.

(Enter TANO.)

TUTU: Hallowed priest of our mighty god—

TANO: What?

TUTU: You are welcome to my palace.

TANO *(curt)*: Indeed.

BOTA: Welcome to the King's palace, mighty One.

TANO: Don't waste my time, young men. Why have you summoned me here?

TUTU: All is not well, mighty One. I need your help, for tragedy pursues your son. Of a truth, you are the thumb without which this land can never tie a knot. You are the foremost teller of oracles of our land. It is only the ant that hears the whispers of the sand. It is only you, mighty One, who can tell the will of the gods. All that is seeable you see, and all that is knowable you know. Were I to mention one by one the wondrous deeds you have done for us, I would talk all day and still not be done.

TANO: Then go straight to the point, I pray you.

TUTU: I have summoned you here, Priest of Tano, because my life is in danger. I am full of fears and do not know what to do now. *(A note of desperation creeping in)* A troubled man am I, and I look forward to my death as nigh and inevitable. I have become derision for my own people, for they think that I am now a madman. I have no peace, mighty One—

TANO *(almost savagely)*: Hold it right there, young man! What is that you said? "Peace"? What peace? Peace is for him whose hands are clean. Oh, how horrible the insanity that leads men to cause trouble beyond their control! How unwise their hearts are! Charge no-one but yourself, Tutu, for your suffering; for you are merely reaping the fruit of the seed you sowed yourself. You killed your brother wrongfully, and, for that reason, the anger of the gods is kindled against you.

(TUTU kneels before him.)

TUTU: Then save me, mighty One! Save me from the anger of the gods. I bow and clasp your knees to beg you… Do save me!

TANO: Why do you supplicate me, young man? With what do you suppose I shall save you? Are you not content with what you have gained? Ashes fly back into the face of him who throws them.

TUTU: I know it well, mighty One, but be merciful to a remorseful man. It is true that I killed my brother— yes, I will not hide it from you. I poisoned him because envy dwelt in my heart. I coveted his crown and throne; I wanted the kingship of the land to be set upon me. But I admit that what I did was abominable, and I repent it sincerely and wholesomely.

TANO: Then accept the punishment thereof, young man.

TUTU: I take refuge in your mercy, mighty One. I bid you importune the gods for me.

(BOTA, too, kneels down.)

BOTA: Do have mercy on the King, companion of the gods. We beg you to intercede with the immortal Ones on his behalf. We know that things hidden from us are naked before your eyes. You are our mouth and our ears to the gods. Therefore we believe that if so be that the gods will be merciful to the King, it is only you who can make that happen. Pray do not hesitate to importune them for him.

TANO: What will be will be, young man. The gods are bent on punishing your king according to the doings of his own hand. A sin against a brother is a sin against the ever-living Ones.

BOTA: That too we know very well, mighty One. Clemency is what we seek from the gods.

TANO: Clemency indeed! Don't forget that the lightning does not know the rain-maker when it strikes.

TUTU *(rising up)*: Don't be headstrong, Priest of Tano. Don't be headstrong, and I shall reward you handsomely. I will give you fifty ingots of gold. I will give you gold dust and women— whatever payment you will ask of me.

TANO *(wrathfully)*: What was that? Gold? Women? Oh you impious wretch! You ought to be ashamed of yourself if there is any shame in you. What do you take me for? A corrupt man? Thank you, but I know better than to sell myself to you for gold and women.

TUTU *(obstinately)*: I know I cannot buy you with gold and women, mighty One. They will merely be a token of my gratitude to you.

TANO: There comes a time, Tutu— and not many days from now—in which you shall be consigned to woeful destruction, and you and your money shall become as filth in the eyes of all who see you today. And oh, what a satisfying sight that shall be!*(Still fiercely)*But now, this is what the gods say I should tell you: Inasmuch as you did what they regard with abhorrence and you felt no remorse for it, they shall make you do what you regard with abhorrence and they will feel no remorse for it. Abomination shall mend what abomination has done. You shall receive a just recompense for your reprehensible deeds. *(Significantly)* In order to preserve your life and appease your brother's spirit, you shall perform what is called ritual coitus. You shall take your own daughter to your marriage-bed, and go into her even as you would to your own wife. After that, you shall take a full-grown, white-horned sheep and, at midnight, bury it beside your brother's grave. When doing this, you shall let no mortal eye see you, lest you lose your sanity. Then you shall after that offer libation to the gods, supplicating for pardon and the preservation of your life. In most solemn truth, your life shall be spared if only you do exactly as I have told you. But if you fail, even to the slightest degree, you shall die when you see your brother's ghost again.

BOTA *(thunderstruck)*: What?

TUTU *(faintly)*: The gods want me to sleep with my own daughter?

BOTA: Upon my word!

TUTU: Isn't that incest, mighty One?

TANO: The gods have spoken, and they must be obeyed.

TUTU: But is that what they want? They want me to sleep with my own daughter? They want me to commit incest?

TANO: If you are not ready to partake of the spirit's food, young man, you don't put your hand into it. No more words and time will I waste.

(He goes off.)

TUTU *(forcibly)*: May it never be! This can nowise be accomplished. I cannot sleep with my— Oh, no! Never!

BOTA: This is serious!

TUTU: Oh, am I not a fool? Am I not a man to be taught a great lesson? I wove a snare for a man and it has caught wind; I dug a pit and I have fallen into it. Oh, Tutu, the ill-fated one, what is this you have done to yourself? O immortal Ones, why? Why do I get this from you? Why do you keep your eyes on me?

BOTA: What do you think now to do, my King?

TUTU: What is there to be done, good friend? Can I add more wrongs to the ones I have already committed? No, I cannot. I simply cannot. If death be my fate, let it come; I do not seek to shun it. I am a murderer, a shedder of brother's blood, and I deserve to die as beseems every murderer.

BOTA: Why do you talk like that, my King? Has the man not told you what needs to be done to escape the punishment?

TUTU *(indignantly)*: What is this, Bota? What are you driving at?

BOTA: My King—

TUTU: So you too want me to commit incest, right? What manner of man are you?

BOTA: My King—

TUTU *(violently)*: Don't win me over, friend! Give it up! Cease enticing me to do what I do not want to do!

BOTA: I am not enticing you to do what you do not want to do, my King. Far be it from to do that! I well know it is better to do nothing than to do an ill. But what I am doing now is not enticing you to do an ill. I am only trying to make you see reason. Just think about it, my King. If you die right now— perish the thought— what will happen to this kingdom, the very reason why you murdered your brother?

TUTU *(tormented)*: Ah! Woe is me!

BOTA: Have you any heir to ascend the throne? Is there any good person like yourself among your kindred to succeed you? Not so.

TUTU: What of it?

BOTA: Then ask yourself— what will happen to your wife, that virtuous keeper of your household?

TUTU *(with a wry smile)*: Listen to that!

BOTA: She will become a widow, banished from all joy and comfort. And your beautiful daughter— is she not the only fruit of your loins? Is she not the apple of your eye? Do spare a thought for them, my King. Think about your wife and daughter. Who will care for them after you are gone? Is it those greedy pot-bellied monsters you have for kinsmen? Don't forget family is like a forest: If you are outside it, it looks dense; but you go inside and see that the trees stand wide apart. *(More eagerly)* Then after your death, what will be on the lips of the people? Think of that too, my King. "He murdered his own brother," thus will they speak, "and now look, the gods have smitten him." Is that the name you want to leave behind you? Don't you want your name to be reverenced after you are gone?

TUTU: Oh, what do the dead care about name, my friend? What do the silent Ones care about posthumous honour? Cease it, fellow, for your speech and inveigling avail not.

BOTA: I will help you, my King.

(TUTU manages a wry laugh.)

TUTU: Are you not funny, Bota? You will help me? How will you help me, tell me? You will come and grip my daughter's legs while I go into her, right?

BOTA: I will give you a potion, my King.

(TUTU stops laughing.)

TUTU: You will do what?

BOTA: Give you a potion. A potion for your daughter to drink before you go into her.

TUTU *(violently)*: And what do you take me for, my friend? The chief of all idiots, huh?

BOTA: My King—

TUTU: So you think I haven't learnt anything yet? You gave me poison to kill my brother and I well-nigh got caught because of that. I even went as far as having an innocent lady put to death, so as to conceal the real facts of the matter. And you are none the wiser!

BOTA: Don't you hold supreme lordship over all the land, my King? Don't you have the utmost liberty to act as you please?

TUTU: And so?

85

BOTA: What I am saying is, you can do to me whatsoever you please if this potion doesn't work as I say it does.

TUTU: I know how your potions work, my friend.

BOTA: I risk my very life on it, my King.

TUTU: Oh, go on— risk the whole world. I don't care.

BOTA: Do not resent my words, my King. It is true that I gave you poison to kill your brother and it nearly landed you in trouble; but, believe me, I don't know how it happened.

TUTU: Nonsensical words!

BOTA: Truly I have no accurate knowledge of how and why the poison betrayed those signs on his body; all the more so because I had not used it myself before. But this potion is different. On sundry occasions have I used it and seen what it is capable of doing. Just a drop of it will deaden your feelings and cause a deep sleep to fall upon you. Nothing can weaken its effect and, trust me, it leaves no signs on the skin. Now if you would so have it, give me leave to get it and lure your daughter to consume it. It takes a long space of time for its effect to wear off, and so you will be able to sleep with her without any difficulty. And what is more, she will never get to know that you slept with her.

TUTU *(flummoxed)*: O gods!

BOTA: Do to me whatever you want if it works contrary to what I have said.

*(Long pause. **TUTU** seems to be in the throes of laborious thought.)*

TUTU: What if this potion not only causes her to sleep, but kills her in the process? Will that not be another murder, another abomination?

BOTA: The potion doesn't kill, my King; it only causes its victims to fall asleep.

TUTU *(Aside)*: Can I do this?

BOTA: Be not in a dilemma, my King. I am not advising you to do something that will bring you trouble.

TUTU: Oh, like I can rely on you!

BOTA: I risk my life on this, my King.

(Pause. **TUTU** *walks to the throne but refuses to sit down.)*

TUTU *(with a sigh))*: Very well then. Now remove all wax from your ears and listen to me, for I mean every word of what I am going to say. I will use the portion of which you have spoken, and follow the course of instruction the Priest of Tano gave me. *(Seriously)*But if the potion works contrary to what you have made me believe it does, not only will I deprive you of your life; I will also make sure your very name is wiped away from the face of the earth. I will raise my fist against your entire household, and sever the root of your kin. I will forget that you ever were my friend and, with evil, repay all the good services you have yielded me. Moreover, I will order your corpse to be impaled on a stick at the entrance of this town as a warning to all who lead others into temptation. And I will sleep with all your daughters, one by one, while coercing them to drink your potion.

BOTA: Be it so, my King. Be it so. *(Aside)* I know what will eventually be mine.

TUTU: Now go, delay not, and bring me the potion. Here will I sit in the meantime. Before you come, put it into something fit to be consumed— soup, wine, or anything— and I will send for my daughter.

BOTA: Sooner said than done, my King.

(He turns to go.)

TUTU: And, Bota—

BOTA: I am here, my King.

TUTU: This is a secret between the two of us.

BOTA: Well-spoken, my King.

(BOTA goes off.)

TUTU: Oh, my heart! My foolish, greedy heart! My unregenerate, deluded heart! What trouble you have caused me! What terrible affliction you have subjected me to! You are cold and given to malice, my heart. You are full of guile and wickedness. You have no regard for me. Were you ever like that in the time past? Oh, no. Then, from where came this inclination to evil, this prostrate submission to wrongdoing?

(He sits on the throne.)

Scene 5

*(*TUTU *sits with his chin in his palms, mumbling to himself. Enter* OBIYAA. *She stands behind him and observes him for a minute.)*

OBIYAA: My husband, why do you sit here talking to yourself? What grief weighs on your mind, my lord?

TUTU: No grief weighs on my mind, woman. I am not mad if that is what you mean to ask. My sanity has not fled me yet.

OBIYAA *(endearingly)*: I have no idea why you are behaving thus, my husband; but I believe there is a good reason for it.

TUTU: Let me ask you a question, Obiyaa. When you came into my bedchamber today, didn't you ask me what was wrong with me? Answer straight.

OBIYAA: I certainly did, my husband.

TUTU: And in reply, what did I say?

OBIYAA: You sat silently on your bed and looked fixedly at me and—

TUTU: Yes, I did all that— but I said something, did I not? What did I open my mouth and say to you?

OBIYAA: You said nothing was wrong with you.

TUTU: Then why? Why do you still worry me? If I told you nothing was wrong with me, why not take my word for it and stop droning into my ears like a mosquito?

OBIYAA *(in an injured tone)*: How could you say something like that to me, my husband? Does it give you no sense of shame to sting me with words? What you did today— or should I say, what befell you today— left no doubt in the minds of the people that their King has now gone mad. They are saying things that are not true. And as

89

your wife, have I no right to inquire of you the truth of the matter? Show me why you are this angry with me.

TUTU: I say there is nothing wrong with me, woman. What else do you want me to say?

OBIYAA *(restrainedly)*: Truly, my husband, it cuts me to the very heart to see you always hiding things from me your wife. You were nothing like that when we married. These days you even speak more to your friends than you do to me.

TUTU: May I know what you want me to say, Obiyaa? You want me to say that I have become sick in the head as everyone is saying, right? Oh, I see! I thought you were my wife. I thought you would doubt it even if everybody said I had gone mad. Now tell me, have you said anything to give me comfort since that incident took place? Any word of solace— have you? Not so. You have done nothing of the sort. In fact, you have done no good by speaking to me since. And here you are trying to taunt me.

OBIYAA: Oh, my husband—

TUTU *(growling)*: Go away from me, woman! Remove yourself from me! I don't want to see your face here again! Go away and leave me be!

OBIYAA: My husband—

TUTU: Go away, I said!

OBIYAA *(sobbingly)*: I obey my husband.

(She curtsies and goes into the palace.)

TUTU: Oh, what is this that I am doing? Why am I now changing into a beast? Do I have to treat my wife this way? She deserves better, she deserves much better. Oh, my heart! My foolish, deluded heart!

(He stands up and begins to pace up and down.)

Scene 6
(Enter BOTA, carrying a bowl of soup.)

BOTA: Look, my King, I have brought it. I have put it in a soup just as you bade me. Now have your daughter fetched here and lure her to consume the soup.

TUTU *(weakly)*: I cannot do it, Bota. I am afraid.

BOTA: Afraid of what, my King?

TUTU: Afraid of everything, my good friend. I am now in a quandary. Whereas my heart tells me that what I am doing is right, my conscience has begun to misgive me. Terrible fear and trembling possess my soul, my mind perplexed concerning right and wrong.

BOTA: Leave this talk, my King. The name of coward never suited you, so quit behaving like one now. Why should you let a sentiment master you? What you are going to do, needless to say, is simple and will cost you nothing. Just summon your daughter and lure her to eat the soup.

TUTU: I say I cannot, good friend.

BOTA: I will go and call her for you, if you cannot.

TUTU *(earnestly)*: Do nothing of the sort, I pray you.

BOTA: Why?

TUTU: She is not your daughter and so you say it as though it is easy—

BOTA: No, it is not easy, my King. I know that you love your daughter heartily and I know how hard this is for you as a father. But is the alternative any better? Ask yourself that question.

TUTU: I cannot do it, Bota. I am a weak person.

BOTA: Stop saying that, my King. You are not a weak person. You, on the contrary, are a lion among men. You are a viper whose venom knows no antidote. I call you the "Iron-hearted Warrior", he who brings his enemies to their knees.

Alter your countenance, high King, for I am going to call your daughter.

(BOTA goes into the palace.)

TUTU: Oh, this weakness in me shall be the cause of my downfall! How do I break its fetters and get my freedom? How do I become a free man? To my silly heart it clings; on my soul it gorges itself. O me!

(Soon OHENEWAA enters.)

OHENEWAA: Father…?

(TUTU starts.)

TUTU *(shakily)*: Oh, Ohenewaa! My princess! My beautifully-browed doll! My chief joy…!

OHENEWAA: What is it, father? Your friend sends word you want to see me.

TUTU: Yes, I do. I sent him to call you for me. *(Affectedly)*Come here, Ohenewaa. Come, my well-beloved! How great is my delight to see you! Now, give your father a hug.

(They hug. OHENEWAA is still in a muddle.)

OHENEWAA: What is the matter, father? Nothing is amiss, I trust?

TUTU: I will tell you that presently, my daughter. But here, seat yourself beside me. You know I am never better pleased than having you by my side.

(OHENEWAA sits down. TUTU tries suppressing his fear.)

OHENEWAA: Is all well?

TUTU: All is well, child. Where is your mother?

OHENEWAA: She is in the kitchen.

TUTU: Doing what?

OHENEWAA: Cooking your evening meal.

TUTU: Oh, all right. *(Shakily)* Have you eaten?

OHENEWAA: No, I have not.

TUTU: Will you not?

OHENEWAA: I don't have the slightest intention of doing so at the moment.

TUTU: True? But you seem weak and hunger-worn.

OHENEWAA: Yes, I know. But after what happened, none of us feels the need to go near food.

TUTU: Oh, listen to that! I am not yet gone and you are abstaining from food on my account. That makes no sense, my daughter. What do I say, then? My house has become a house of mourning because I am more like a dead man now. Such is not what I want, my dear. Come on, get you something to eat. I have kept some soup in that bowl for you. Take it and appease your hunger. *(Aside)* Oh, what am I doing?

OHENEWAA: Thank you, father, but I feel not like eating now.

TUTU: Don't say that, child. I am your father; when I give you food, I expect you to eat it without question.

OHENEWAA *(beseechingly)*: Oh why, father?

TUTU: Oh why? I begot you, Ohenewaa; it is my responsibility to give you food to eat. And it will be a sign of disrespect on your part, my dear, if you refuse this or any other food I give you.

OHENEWAA: I believe you said that in jest, didn't you?

TUTU: Many a true word is spoken in jest, my daughter. *(Threateningly)* Take the soup and eat!

OHENEWAA: All right, father. It seems you will take it much to heart if I refuse to eat this soup. I will take just a mouthful of it and make you happy.

TUTU: Do, my daughter. *(Aside)*Oh, it is more profitable for me to throw myself into the jaws of a leopard! Why am I doing this to her? She is an innocent girl.

(OHENEWAA uncovers the bowl and brings out a piece of meat.)

OHENEWAA *(with glee)*: It is venison!

TUTU *(guiltily)*: You like venison?

OHENEWAA: Very much.

TUTU: You see, I know your favourite.

OHENEWAA: Thank you, father.

TUTU *(aside)*: Don't thank me, child. Take an axe and hack your father into pieces.

(OHENEWAA begins to eat the soup; TUTU seems ill at ease.)

OHENEWAA: Mother was shedding tears in the kitchen, father. Were you fighting with her?

TUTU: Fighting? By no means, my dear. It was just a little misunderstanding between us.

OHENEWAA: And she was shedding tears?

TUTU: You know your mother: she has an aptitude for exaggerating matters.

(Silence. OHENEWAA continues to eat.)

OHENEWAA: I have made a resolution, father.

TUTU: What is it?

OHENEWAA *(tongue-in-cheek)*: I am not going to marry.

TUTU *(surprised albeit uneasy)*: You are certain of it? And whatever could have put such a thought into my dear daughter's head?

OHENEWAA: I want my life to be merry and peaceful, father, without even a speck of pain and sorrow. Marriage, to me, is a plague. Better a lovelorn spinster than a regretful wife. More often than not, I ask myself: Why should a man and a woman, in spite of their adverse characters, aptitudes, and temperaments, come to dwell under one roof for the remainder of their days? It is just burdensome.

TUTU: By the spirits, Ohenewaa, what an artless child you are! Likewise was I wont to think when I was your age. With your green years, to be sure, there are so many things you will always be wrong-headed about. Age makes us better knowers of truth and better solvers of mysteries. Marriage is not as bad as it seems to you. It is an honour, not a plague. Our elders say that, "A woman without a husband is like a body without a head…"

OHENEWAA *(continuing the proverb)*:"… and a man without a wife is like a head without a body." I have heard it many times.

TUTU: You are a remarkable child, my dear, but wisdom comes with length of days. Your life is now in bud and blade— you will understand some things better when you attain womanhood.

OHENEWAA *(aside)*: I will not tell him I have already begun puberty, lest he hale me into an early marriage. I will ask mother not to tell him also.

TUTU *(elegiac)*: Be attentive and listen to what I tell you, daughter. Today you are few of days and know nothing about the austerity of life. But very soon you shall come to the full measure of your prime, and everybody will call you woman. When that time comes, I want you to be a cat.

OHENEWAA *(at sea)*: A cat?

TUTU: Whereas men are cats, women are dogs. A cat sees something and winks at it. But a dog sees the self-same thing and barks at it all day. Such advice I give you, don't be like those dogs.

OHENEWAA *(smiling)*: I hear you, father. I will be a cat.

TUTU: Good to hear that! *(Becoming emotional)* Mightily do I love you, Ohenewaa. Nobody beneath the sun shall be more beloved of me than you. That's why I always seek the best for you. Now you are young and ripe in beauty; when you reach your womanhood, I want you to be a strong woman of virtuous character— rich in wit and full of mental energy. Don't be perplexed why I am saying all this, my dear. For I am doing so to show you how well-minded I am towards you. I am solicitous about your future, my daughter. I recall vividly the day you came out of your mother's womb, how I insisted on beholding your face even when the women who helped your mother in childbirth said it was not good for me to do so. I remember I swathed you in a fine cloth and dandled you in my arms. And do you know what I said?

OHENEWAA: Tell me, father.

TUTU: I said, "This child will make me cry."

OHENEWAA: You did? And why did you say that?

TUTU: Patience, my daughter. I will tell you soon. We are going to the city of birds— no need to pick birds' nests on the way.

OHENEWAA: There is too much pepper in the soup, father.

TUTU: Oh… let me get you some water. *(Calling)* Maid! Maid!

(One of the Maids enters from the palace.)

MAID *(curtsying)*: I heard my Lord calling.

TUTU: Make haste and fetch water for the Princess.

MAID: Very well, my Lord.

(She goes into the palace.)

TUTU: Have you finished eating the soup?

OHENEWAA: No, but that is all I will eat.

TUTU: You enjoyed it?

OHENEWAA: Very much, despite the fact that there is too much pepper in it.

(Re-enter MAID with water.)

TUTU: Give it to the Princess.

(OHENEWAA drinks the water.)

OHENEWAA: Thank you.

TUTU: Is the hotness reduced now?

OHENEWAA: No, but I think it will.

TUTU: That will be all, maid. Now take the calabash and go inside.

(MAID goes back to the palace.)

OHENEWAA: I feel sleepy, father.

TUTU *(aside)*: Ah, time for yet another abomination!

OHENEWAA *(drowsily)*: What were you saying?

TUTU: Now to continue what I was saying, Ohenewaa, let me tell you why I said, "This child will make me cry." Just think about it, my dear; you are blessed as no other girl in this land is blessed. You have been endowed with great beauty by the Creator and have a very great family. He who begot you is King and she who brought you forth is the most loving of mothers. There is a saying that, if a man is great, even his dog wears a proud look. You have every good reason to wear a proud look, my daughter, for you are more blessed than you could ever have imagined. However, very soon things will change. And don't get me wrong, my dear, when I say things will change. What I mean to say is that, soon your puberty will come and you shall be ushered into womanhood, fit for wedlock. Then shall come to me a young man who has regal blood in his veins like yourself, and ask for your hand in marriage. As per our custom, he shall pay your bride-price and give me your head-drink to seal the union. After that, he shall claim you his and bear you away from this house, forever keeping you as his wife. On that day, I will shed many tears for losing my much-loved daughter. I shall not see you as that bundle of joy that made me smile on the day of its birth. Thus explains why I said, "This child will make me cry." Now I believe you understand me?

(No answer; OHENEWAA is fast asleep.)

Ohenewaa! My princess! Jewel of my palace!

(No answer. He touches her.)

Ohenewaa, are you asleep? Can you hear me?

(No answer. He stands up.)

O you guests of air that hover over me, and you haters of good that rumble beneath me, you who permit evil to make its dwelling in the bosoms of men, twirling them hither and thither till they do your bidding, pray come to me! Come to me, invisible Ones, come and permit me to drink my fill of your deviltry. Such as you are, Spirits, take possession of my heart and use me. Use me, for my strength is meagre.

(He checks again if she is asleep.)

Ohenewaa! My well-beloved!

(No answer. He carries her in his arms and enters his bedchamber.)

CURTAIN.

Act III

As in the beginning of the Second Act, the stage is in complete darkness after the ascension of the curtain. Nothing has changed.

Scene 1

The spotlight falls and reveals **TANO** *who is now dressed as one of the servants of the King's palace. He smiles knowingly at us and, as usual, comes forward to address us:*

TANO: Five moons have gone by since Tutu got the title of King.
I, Tano, the first-begotten of Odomankoma,
came to this land to tell him what he needed to do
to escape the punishment of his misdeeds,
only to make sure that the very act by which he thought
to save himself was the cause of his ruin.
Now Tutu is at ease and about as happy as a mortal man can be.
But that is destined to be short-lived.
For today I have come to his palace in the shape and likeness
of one of his own servants, to ensure that
the punishment visited upon him is brought to its utmost degree.
And not only that. From here,
I shall put off this guise of a palace servant
and re-assume the form of my priest,
to reveal to all the people of this land

the evil that their King did and the wages it has earned him.

(Presently, **TUTU** *enters and sees* **TANO**.)

TUTU: Hey, you there! What are you doing?

TANO: I am doing nothing, your Majesty.

TUTU: Oh, fools and lazybones in my palace! I don't know why I still have people like you in my employ. Be quick now, fool; go call Bota here without delay. Tell him to stop whatever he is doing and come.

TANO: Did you say Bota, your Majesty?

TUTU: Were you sleeping when I was talking?

TANO: You mean Bota your friend, your Majesty?

TUTU: And how many Botas do you know in this town?

TANO: Three, my Lord.

TUTU: And they are…?

TANO: I know Bota the blacksmith.

TUTU: Yes?

TANO: I know Bota the woodcarver.

TUTU: And who else…?

TANO: And the last one is Bota, the man who normally comes here. Is he the one your Majesty would like to see?

TUTU: Oh, stupid man! What is your name?

TANO: My name is Esum.

TUTU: You are the rankest fool I have ever seen. Thank your lucky stars that I'm in a good mood today, or I would have cut off your brainless head and fed it to vultures.

TANO: I pray your Majesty's pardon.

TUTU: Just shut up, my friend! Cease saying things to flare up my anger. And now listen. I am spitting on the ground. If my saliva dries up before the man comes to the palace, you will wish yourself dead.

TANO: Very well, your Majesty.

(Exit **TANO**.)

100

(TUTU goes to the throne and sits down. Enter OBIYAA.)

OBIYAA: May I trouble my lord for a moment?

TUTU: What is it?

OBIYAA: There is something I wish to talk to you about if no duty requires your attention at the moment.

TUTU: Speak, I am listening.

OBIYAA: It is about our daughter, my lord.

TUTU *(trying not to appear frightened)*: What now?

OBIYAA: I think there is something wrong with her, my lord. She has started behaving in a very strange way and I can't figure her out. Nowadays she doesn't eat, she doesn't sleep, she doesn't speak to anybody, and, from morning to evening, she immures herself in her bedchamber.

TUTU *(affectation of nonchalance)*: Oh, really? She is sick, wouldn't you say?

OBIYAA: For some time now, she has been going to the back of the house; so I thought it might be attributable to some pubertal problems.

TUTU *(shocked)*: You mean Ohenewaa has reached puberty?

OBIYAA: Yes, my lord.

TUTU *(joy in his voice)*: And you haven't told me? Don't you know her puberty rite must be performed?

OBIYAA: I do, my lord. But I wanted to study her for some time, as is right. Sometimes what we see may not be an initial menstrual flow, and so we take our time to study them.

TUTU: And have you inquired of her what is it that is ailing her now?

OBIYAA: Yes, I have.

TUTU: And what did she say?

OBIYAA: She said it was a slight fever.

TUTU: And what have you done about it? This slight fever?

OBIYAA: I have boiled some herbs for her to drink, my lord, but I see no change in her. She still doesn't eat— still keeps herself to herself.

TUTU: Go boil more herbs for her to drink. Gradually recovery will come to her. And when you are giving her the medicine, don't forget to give her something to eat as well. You know the herbs can't take away the malady if her stomach is empty.

OBIYAA: I will do so without fail, my lord.

(Exit **OBIYAA**.*)*

TUTU: Oh, good tidings! A balm to my soul! My daughter has reached her puberty… which means I can now give her hand in marriage to a man. That will I do with alacrity. Indeed, what I did to her— or should I say, what the priest made me do to her— seems to haunt my conscience with guilt . I will have no peace of mind as long as she is in this house. Last night I dreamt a dream about her. It was a dreadful dream that spoilt my rest and filled my bosom with trepidation. In it, I saw her pointing a dagger at me while blood oozed out of her eyes. Although I am no interpreter of dreams, I daresay such a dream is an ill omen. But sorry, my daughter; I never meant to do that to you. Your father had no choice.

(Enter **BOTA,** *who stops and bows in a gesture of greeting as soon as he sees* **TUTU**.*)*

BOTA: Ah, very true, very true!
It is the living man who causes the denizen
of the spirit world to long for mashed yam!

TUTU *(pleased to see him)*: Bota my brother!

BOTA: I say it is very true that
he who has seen a thousand, praises not a hundred.

Adu Tutu, you have seen a thousand—
tens of thousands—
and so a hundred is nothing to you.
Oh, is it not wonderful
that the snake that only crawls and does not fly,
has caught the hornbill whose home is in the sky?
If the wind can lift up a stone,
then take care of yourself if you are a small light gourd.
Adu Tutu, the raging fire,
Adu Tutu, the *ofuntum* tree that breaks the axe,
he who eats palm-nut soup with the right hand,
bending low with humility, I greet you.

TUTU: Your greeting is well received, Bota. I trust you are doing well today?

BOTA: If you are well, I am well, my King.

TUTU: Oh, good to hear that. Come, come, come. Do seat yourself.

(BOTA sits down.)

BOTA: I was about to put something into my belly when your servant came and told me you would like to see me at once. Why? Is anything wrong?

TUTU: All is well, Bota.

BOTA: Then what is it? *(Humorously)* To what especial circumstance may I be indebted for this call?

TUTU: I was thinking this morning, my good friend, about the things that have befallen me in recent times. And I did realize something. *(Pleasantly)* Now I am King and have obtained great power in my hand. I rule these people who look up to me with reverence as great as that with which they look up to the gods. I possess vast wealth and my fame has been bruited abroad over all the lands. As a matter of fact, I am now tremendously happy and lack nothing of all that I desire in this life. But if a dog is found up on a kitchen shelf and could not have climbed up himself, then someone must have lifted him and put him there. The truth is, I could not entirely have obtained all these things without your help, Bota. To you do I owe all that I am today. False friends are like a shade: you see them only when the sun is shining. But you have not been like that. To me you have been a true friend in both good times and ill. In deeds whereby I have deserved severe punishment or even death, you have always been close and helpful. And so I asked myself, "How do I requite all that Bota has done for me? How do I express my gratitude to him in kind?" I tried and cudgelled my brain, only I couldn't for the life of me come up with anything good enough. Therefore I have sent for you and want you to tell me yourself. Tell me the height of your wishes and I shall grant it without delay.

BOTA *(aside)*: Oh, long-awaited words! It has happened just as I wanted. But lest he call me a sycophant, I must first feign reluctance.

TUTU: Say it, Bota. I want to show you a kindness. That is why I bade my servant call you for me.

BOTA: May you be great for ever, my King!

TUTU: So may it be.

BOTA: May abundance of blessings abide on you for what you have done today.

TUTU: Much obliged.

BOTA: Truth be told, my King, you have proved to me today that you are a man of great wisdom. For he is especially a fool who gets to the top of a tree and eats its fruit without passing down some to the one who pushed him to get there. I have done a lot for you, it is true, and well have you done by showing your appreciation for it. Nevertheless, it would speak ill of me if I asked anything in return as you bid me. You are more than a friend to me and I deem serving you as a reward in itself.

TUTU: You have spoken well, Bota, but you have said nothing to convince me. By your help and loyalty, you have me a grateful man. My father always said something and never will I forget it. He said, "Verily, dogs don't prefer bones to meat; they like bones only because nobody gives them meat." And I find that saying to be much true. I for one know you for an intensely ambitious man, a man who has an ardent thirst for heroic deeds. For oftentimes have I heard you speak with such extravagant enthusiasm about the things you would like to achieve if only you had the chance. Now I, your friend, have been made King; my wealth is beyond measure and I do things as I will. If any man can help you fulfil those ambitions of yours, I can. Therefore say it and don't hide it.

BOTA: My King, you well know the manner of person I am. I, as a rule, don't like asking favours from others. For I am no dog that wags its tail at men because of their food. If I offer you help, I do so from an inward principle— call it, the wellspring of an altruistic nature. Nothing have I done for your Majesty with an ulterior motive. That notwithstanding, I shall make a request, seeing that you are steadfastly determined to show me your gratitude. But before I do so, permit me to remind you of something you seem to have forgotten.

TUTU: What is it, good friend?

BOTA: It is true that you have been made King and been given the supreme power of the land. But do remember that, not all are asleep who have their eyes closed. There are people around you— and numerous are they— who hate your kingship and would stop at nothing to see you fall. We say that, it is only the dead man who has no enemies. But the fact is, when there are no enemies within, we need not fear those without.

TUTU *(nervously)*: Your words are true, but I haven't rightly taken your meaning. Pray go straight to the point.

BOTA: What I am trying to say, my King, is that, your Chiefs, those men whose duty it is to assist you in the governance of this land, are not worthy of your trust. They conceive a jealousy at your elevation and are very crafty in their design against you. Indeed, they are the very ones who go about speaking injuriously of you and turning the hearts of your own subjects against you. Therefore this is my request: make me a Chief and a member of your council. Let me be vested with power to make decisions with you, so that you will enjoy peaceful kingdom. Together, let us thwart the evil schemes of your enemies and strengthen your hand on the people. That is my request, my King.

(TUTU stands up, smiles nervously, paces up and down for a moment, and gives a nod of appreciation.)

TUTU: Like always, my good friend, you have spoken much to my liking. You never miss a trick, do you? A right word you have said to me. The Tortoise says, it is for fear of what tomorrow may bring that makes him carry his shell wherever he goes. I will do as you have counselled me. Not only will it be a fitting token of my gratitude to you, but also a strategic measure to safeguard my kingship.

BOTA *(eagerly)*: Do as you have spoken, my King.

TUTU *(calling)*: Guard! Guard!

(Enter TANO from the palace, running.)

TANO: Here am I, my Lord.

TUTU: Go to the homes of all the Chiefs and inform them that I want to see them straightway.

TANO: I obey my Lord.

(He goes off, running.)

TUTU: Come, Bota. My wife set my dining table a while ago. Let us go inside and eat something before those men come.

(Both of them go into the palace.)

SCENE 2

(One of the doors opens and **OHENEWAA** *and* **MAID** *enter, carrying eggs and wine.)*

OHENEWAA *(languidly)*: I would desire another request of you, maid.

MAID: Ready am I to do whatever my Princess commands.

OHENEWAA: Go to my bedchamber and look under my bed. You shall see a piece of cloth in which are wrapped all my formal clothes. Untie it and pick out the one that seems the most beautiful to you. Put it on my bed and get all the marching accessories for it from my jewel box. Then go to the slaves' quarters and get me one of the women there who is most skilled in plaiting hair. After that, go to the kitchen and cook plantain and *kontomire* stew— just the way I like it. Set the table for one, and come and call me.

MAID: I hear you, my Princess.

OHENEWAA *(gently)*: I shall come inside very shortly.

(MAID walks to the door and turns back.)

MAID: Before that, my Princess…

OHENEWAA: Yes?

MAID: May I ask you something?

OHENEWAA: Be not afraid to do so. What is it?

MAID: Of late, my Princess, I have been observing you as you go and come in this palace. Long have I watched you rejecting all conversation and keeping yourself to yourself. You don't eat, you don't sleep… it seems you have been excessively grieved. Pray tell me, my Princess, what is the matter?

OHENEWAA: At whose behest are you asking me this question? My mother's?

MAID: No, my Princess.

OHENEWAA: Then whose?

MAID: I am concerned about you as much as your mother, my Princess. You know the King has entrusted you to my keeping. And, besides, I am a mother myself. I have given birth to seven children from this belly of mine. Therefore, if I see you not looking yourself, I feel it is my maternal duty to know what the problem is.

(Profound silence. **OHENEWAA** *keeps her eyes down.)*

OHENEWAA *(silently)*: Is there any human being who fears not to unfold their secret where it may not be kept, good maid? I am a mortal being like you. On one condition will I disclose to you the pains within the recesses of my breast: I want you to swear that you will never reveal it to anybody as long as there is breath in your nostrils.

MAID: My Princess' secret shall go with me to my grave.

OHENEWAA *(thickly)*: No, that is not how I want it to be. Come here… this is a shrine. Kneel before it and swear… let the gods bear witness. Swear to them that if you dare so much as breathe a word of this secret to any living mortal, they should strike you and even kill you.

*(***MAID** *kneels before the household shrine to swear.)*

MAID: May the mighty gods strike me dead and even let me die accursed if I tell my Princess' secret to any human being.

OHENEWAA: Very good. Now I will tell you the truth, all without concealment.

MAID: Do so, my Princess.

OHENEWAA: It is indeed as you have said, maid: nowadays I haven't being myself. I shrink from food, I shrink from conversation, I love solitude. But that is not without a good reason. *(Significantly)* It all began on the day my father called me to pass the time of day with him in front of the palace. I wouldn't say it was unlike him to do something like that, but I was completely baffled by his actions. He gave me a bowlful of soup to eat and struck up a conversation with me. He spoke verbosely about how much he loved me and wanted me to behave when I had come to womanhood. After eating the soup— I don't know what happened— a deep sleep overmastered me and I saw nothing again. I might have slept for a long time, for when the sleep fell from my eyes, I realized that I was lying in my bedchamber, instead of sitting beside my father. And what did I see upon my waking up? I saw that I had been deflowered.

MAID *(shocked)*: Gods of our land! Deflowered?

OHENEWAA: Somebody had lain with me and, alas, I didn't know how it had happened. I saw blood and felt pains in my pubic regions. For fear of being scorned and scolded, I couldn't bring myself to tell anybody— not even the very woman whose womb gave me life. But four months after that, I have found out that I am no more menstruating. And worse than that, I have found out that I am now with child.

MAID *(terror-stricken)*: You are what? You are with child? Oh, our ancestors!

(OHENEWAA begins to cry.)

OHENEWAA: I have broken a taboo of our land and only the gods know what will happen to me. Since that unutterable day, I have known no peace and my life has become an intolerable burden for me. Day and night alike, I weep and subject myself to pangs of hunger by reason of the terrible grief in my heart. My stomach detests the look of food and my eyes can't get a single wink of sleep. Everything seems to hold terror for me, and my departure from this cold world seems close. Such, if you wish to know, good maid, is the truth and the whole truth behind my recent behaviour.

MAID *(with bona fide compassion)*: Oh, my Princess, my heart throbs as though it would leap out of my bosom as I listen to your sorry tale. Of a truth, I knew there was a problem, but never did I expect it to be of such magnitude. We both know the profoundly terrible consequences of a girl becoming pregnant before her puberty rite is performed among our people. Not only is it a shame to her kinsfolk, but a taboo punishable by lifetime banishment or even death.

OHENEWAA: I know.

MAID: But take heart, my Princess. I am positive that there's a solution to this. What you need to do now is to bide your time and we'll see what we can do.

OHENEWAA: I hear you, maid. I find solace in your words. Thank you.

(A pregnant pause.)

MAID: And if I may ask, my Princess, since the day you learnt that you had been deflowered, have you been able to summon enough courage to ask your father anything concerning it?— To learn truth of the matter?

OHENEWAA: I have not, and I will not.

MAID: Oh, may the gods forefend what I am thinking!

(Another pregnant pause.)

OHENEWAA: The man cannot even look me in the eye nowadays when he sees me.

MAID: I reserve my judgment, my Princess, for the man is your father.

OHENEWAA *(firmly)*: Whether he is or not, I will do what I have to do.

MAID: I don't understand, my Princess.

OHENEWAA: You see these eggs and wine in my hands? I have brought them to the shrine to seek to the gods and invoke a curse on the man who did this to me. I want the gods to bring him to an open shame and cause him to suffer even as I am suffering.

MAID: May the ever-living Ones listen to you, my Princess. May they deal bitterly with him, whoever he may be.

OHENEWAA: Thank you, maid. Now I pray you, go and do what I asked of you.

MAID: Consider it all done, my Princess.

(MAID exits. **OHENEWAA** *slowly kneels before the shrine and holds the eggs up to pray.)*

OHENEWAA: Hear me, O Odomankoma; hear me, Mother Earth; hear me, Tano and your fellow gods. To your hallowed shrine have I come, to seek justice and revenge. I am here, for I am deep in woe... and, Oh, shame chases after me like a lion. My heart is filled with terror, and the grave— the grave seems to be the only answer to my grief. For I, an unmarried girl, have broken a taboo among my people. I'm pregnant and don't know how it happened. However, from you gods nothing can be hidden. For you are divine and everything man does is naked before your eyes. You reward the good and punish the evil; you put to shame doers of evil and expose their designs. Why then do you watch this enormity of wickedness against me and do nothing about it? Why do you let the author of this unspeakable deed have peace while I sink under this weight of sorrow? Can you find no compassion in your heart for a dying girl? Do you feel nothing for her who has been victimized? In my hands I carry eggs and wine, immortal Ones, not to render thanks nor ask for prosperity from you. Rather, I've come to offer a prayer of evil and lay a curse on the man who uncovered my nakedness and made me pregnant. If you are correctly called gods and will never let any evil go unpunished, mercifully listen to my cry and avenge with due vengeance this evil he did against me. Let him be like an ownerless dog and let a fate, such that no man can withstand, overtake him. Deprive him of his substance, his name, his wife, and his offspring. Cause him to come to a most shameful end and be a victim of ridicule everywhere he goes. *(With more pain)* And now, gods, if my royal father, the man who begot me, is this same man I am cursing, then let this and even worse come upon him if he so much as sheds a tear on account of my death. Let him lose his sanity and his throne if he weeps and mourns me. Let him be a scavenger among his own people, and let all men learn a lesson from his fall. Do accept this oblation, immortal Ones, and answer my prayer.

(She pours the wine and smashes the eggs on the ground. Then she goes back into the palace. The flute is heard in the background, adding gravity to what just happened.)

Scene 3
(CHIEFS enter from offstage.)

THIRD CHIEF: Never before has the King summoned us in the same manner as he has done today. The messenger bade me haste forth with all speed. What is the matter?

FOURTH CHIEF: I was even about to take my bath when the messenger came. I had to put my water somewhere and run to this place.

SECOND CHIEF: Let's wait to hear it from the man himself. Whatever it is, I see it not to be a small matter.

(They sit down.)

FIRST CHIEF: Look at the face of the sky... no sign of rain.

SECOND CHIEF: I don't think it will rain within this month.

THIRD CHIEF: Things have changed, brothers. Things are not working well these days.

FOURTH CHIEF: It seems the gods are angry with us.

THIRD CHIEF: And why shouldn't they be? Can you ask for palm oil with a gourd that has no opening?

CHIEFS: Impossible!

(Enter TUTU and BOTA. In token of respect, CHIEFS stand up.)

TUTU: Sit down, Chiefs. I bid you a hearty welcome to my palace.

CHIEFS: Thank you, your Majesty.

(They all sit.)

TUTU: I am glad to see you all honouring my call with such alacrity. As they say, a tree doesn't move this way or that if there is no wind. I have a good reason for summoning you.

CHIEFS: We are listening, your Majesty.

TUTU: The reason is simple. *(Clears his throat.)* Let me begin by saying that a King is like a chicken. He is like a chicken, whereas his Chiefs are like the feathers of the chicken. If the feathers are beautiful, the chicken is beautiful. If the feathers are ugly, the chicken is ugly. What do I mean by that? As King of the land, I have you as my Chiefs. You are holders of high offices of state and it's your duty to assist me in the administration of affairs. You are supposed to guard me and make me look good in the eyes of the people. If I am taking the right path, you have every right to tell me I am taking the right path. So also, if I am taking the wrong path, you are well within your right to tell me I am taking the wrong path. You are never wrong to show me wherein I err when I am discharging my duties as King. For there is truth in what our elders say: He who is creating the path cannot tell if it is crooked.

CHIEFS: That is true!

TUTU: A King without good counsellors is like a blind wayfarer heading towards a ditch. In order to enjoy a prosperous kingdom, every king must be guarded by men of good sense and prudence. I am talking about men endued with profound wisdom and perfect judgment, men worthy of the King's trust. Therefore it is not out of place for him, the King, to make or unmake someone a Chief. In fact, it is for that reason our tradition demands that a Chief swear an allegiance to the King upon his instalment as chief.

CHIEFS: Very true!

TUTU: And so, it is neither out of place nor contrary to precedent for me too, as King of the land, to make or unmake someone a Chief. As a matter of fact, I summoned this council because I want to make someone a Chief today. And this person is none other than my own long-time friend, Bota, who is here with us. We all know Bota in this town; we know the combination of traits he possesses. He is a man both brave and industrious, both unblemished in character and well-versed in the ways of our people. Today I've decided to make him a Chief, so that, like you, he shall be able to assist me for the general good of our people. Now I should like, before proceeding any further, to know you views on this.

(CHIEFS whisper together. Then SECOND CHIEF stands up and bows to the King.)

SECOND CHIEF: Your Majesty, I have listened to your brilliant words and in nothing you said can I contradict you. Truly, it is a truth as familiar to me as it is to you that your bosom friend Bota is a very good son of our land. There is no gainsaying the nobility of his character, and, as you rightly said, he is well-versed in the ways of our people. Therefore, if you delight to make him a Chief, I for one have no objection to it.

(Sits down.)

TUTU: Well-spoken!

THIRD CHIEF *(getting up)*: Your Majesty, our wise men have a saying: If we know a man at daytime, we don't light a lamp at night-time to look at his face.

TUTU: True!

THIRD CHIEF: Bota is no stranger to us; we know him like the very palms of our hands. And I must say that he is every bit as good as you said of him; we all bear testimony to that fact. With all his meek heart he has served your Majesty and been firm in his loyalty to this throne. Therefore it will be a fitting honour done him if the King makes him a Chief and a member of this council. I am in complete agreement with you, my King; that honour will be worthy of him.

(Sits down.)

TUTU: Good words!

FOURTH CHIEF *(getting up)*: Your Majesty, I am of the same mind as my brothers. They have spoken truly. Bota has proved himself a good son of the land and, for that reason, deserves to be honoured in whatever way the King deems fit. It is said that, we send the wise child, and not the long-legged child. Bota is not a long-legged child, but a wise child who has shown exceptional perspicacity in all that he does. Therefore, if your Majesty wants to bestow on him any royal honour, I cannot take exception to it.

(Sits down.)

TUTU: Well-spoken! *(To* **FIRST CHIEF***)* I haven't heard you proffer your opinion, old one. You are always the first to speak.

FIRST CHIEF *(getting up)*: Your Majesty, and brother-members of council, in fact, I didn't want to say anything about the foregoing discussion. For it is always difficult to throw a stone at a lizard that clings to a pot. But since your Majesty urges me to declare my mind to council, I'll do so, even at the risk of displeasing all of you. I know it is so of a truth that the man of whom we speak is a very good friend of the King's. Therefore it is not surprising at all, at least to me, that the King has a mind to show him this honour. Our elders say that, between good friends, even water drunk is sweet enough. Yes, friendship can be stronger than kinship. We have seen some before. *(Pause.)*I know Bota very well, for his father was like a brother to me. Nevertheless, that will not prevent me from speaking as my mind bids me; for we don't beat the side of a drum if its head is there. I listened with scarcely a breath of sound when the King was speaking; and to you too, my brothers, I listened with great attention, when you were speaking. And indeed, if every word you said about Bota is worthy of belief, then I

116

must say that he is a man of very noble character. But is that the only reason why the King desires to do him this honour? If so, I take exception to it. For there are many men in this town who possess by far nobler character, men who merit the good favours of your Majesty, and yet have not so much as been summoned to the royal palace before. It is indeed a glaring truth none here can deny, that the King wants to honour Bota only because of their friendship. If my King verily wants my opinion, then he should listen to me and resent not what I am about to tell him. The position and power of a Chief is not a piece of jewellery that it can be wrapped up and be given to a friend as a gift. If your Majesty wants his reign to be healthy and peaceful, he should follow the path of his ancestors. He should avoid favouritism shown to friends and, as is meet, render honour to them whom honour is due. I am done speaking.

(He sits down. Foreseeing an outburst of anger, **CHIEFS** *begin to whisper among themselves.)*

TUTU: Let me ask you a question, old man. Do you know why the owl is regarded as the wisest of all birds?

FIRST CHIEF: On my honour, I don't know, your Majesty.

TUTU *(with towering contempt)*: And yet you call yourself a Chief? Well, I'll tell you. The owl is regarded as the wisest of all birds because the more it sees, the less it speaks. A flow of words is no proof of wisdom; for wise men know it is better to stumble with the feet than to stumble with the mouth. Like always, what you just said is impetuous and barren of wit— no better than the words of a child. It seems that in age you are much advanced, but in wisdom you are just a laggard. Perhaps you've been afflicted with failings of the mind by reason of your age, and you ought not to brag about being wise. And perhaps you thought wisdom was the

117

prerogative of the elderly and so whatever you said would be accepted in council. If so, old man, you are quite mistaken. If beards were all, the he-goat would be King.

SECOND CHIEF: I pray your Majesty, those are very offensive words.

TUTU: "Very offensive"? Nonsense! Do I need kindly words to tell the man that he is a fool?

THIRD CHIEF: Such is not seemly, your Majesty.

TUTU *(petulantly)*: Oh, go on! Defend him! Say more to justify his foolishness! Is it not the fetishes that show the fetish priest how to turn when dancing? I know you are all behind this.

FOURTH CHIEF: We are not, your Majesty. But—

TUTU *(thundering)*: But what?

FOURTH CHIEF: You know he merely expressed his opinion as is his right in council. He meant well and was guided by no wrong motives. And as our King, it ill behoves you to—

TUTU: "As our King"? Listen to that! Oh, I see! All animals can run, but if the cow runs people say it is mad. Because I am your King, do I have to keep quiet if a man is fooling? What right has he to tell me whom to honour and whom not to honour? Tell me.

CHIEFS: That's not what we are saying, your Majesty.

(FIRST CHIEF stands up.)

FIRST CHIEF: I beg your Majesty—

TUTU: What?

FIRST CHIEF *(kneeling)*: If I injured my King's feelings in my speech, I pray for his pardon. I am very sorry, your Majesty, your servant wasn't thinking. I spoke unbecomingly and now take back every word I uttered. The wisdom of a slave is in his master's head. I can never know better than you. *(Bowing low)* If you desire to make Bota a

Chief, my King, I give my unreserved approval to your decision.

(A moment of silence.)

SECOND CHIEF: Forgive him, your Majesty. He has retracted his words.

THIRD CHIEF: He will not do that again, your Majesty.

FOURTH CHIEF: He has agreed to your decision without demur.

TUTU *(unappeased)*: Perhaps I have not behaved like a leopard and now everybody is calling me a civet-cat. Perhaps I have not been using my royal power and you people take me for a weakling. I must do something to show you all that I am King. If I say yes, nobody can say no.

(As they are talking, **GUARD** *enters, running.)*

GUARD: Your Majesty... O, your Majesty!

TUTU: Speak, for goodness' sake!

GUARD: I bring you evil tidings, your Majesty!

TUTU: What is it?

GUARD: It is Ohenewaa, your Majesty. She has taken her own life!

TUTU: What?

GUARD: The Princess... she has taken her own life! In her bedchamber!

TUTU: O gods, let it not be! Let it not be!

(TUTU and **BOTA** *run into the palace.)*

FIRST CHIEF *(to* **GUARD***)*: Come closer, young man. What you told the King, tell us also.

GUARD: I brought the tidings of the Princess' death, my lord. She has committed suicide inside her bedchamber.

CHIEFS: O gods!

FIRST CHIEFS: Did you, young man, with your own eyes see the Princess dead, or are you telling us something reported?

GUARD: With this pair of eyes I saw her, my lord. Her yet-warm body suspended at the end of a rope.

FIRST CHIEF: Tell me this. Who was the first person to see her dead? Were you the one or was it one of the court attendants? This I ask out of concern; for I fear Tutu might repeat the mistake he, frantic with vexation, made on the day his brother died.

GUARD: I wasn't the first person to see her dead, neither was it any of the court attendants.

FIRST CHIEF: Who then?

GUARD: The Princess was first seen by Obiyaa, her own mother.

SECOND CHIEF *(shaking the head)*: O unhappy woman, she!

THIRD CHIEF: So great is the grief that will consume her! Her only child gone just like that!

FOURTH CHIEF: She is now bereft of all motherly joys. May the gods give her the strength to endure her pains.

FIRST CHIEF: And young man—

GUARD: My lord?

FIRST CHIEF: Has it been ascertained why the Princess did this unspeakable thing to herself?

GUARD: In fact, my lord, nobody knows why she did that to herself.

FIRST CHIEF: There has to be a valid reason.

SECOND CHIEF: I am with you there, brother. There has to be a valid reason.

GUARD *(after a pause)*: I don't know the whole story, my lords, but I shall try and in brief unfold to you what my ears have caught. They say recently the King's daughter was behaving in a very unusual way. If the rumours be true, she looked like a woman with child.

CHIEFS *(mouths agape)*: Eh?

GUARD: But those who saw it were not bold enough to tell it to the King or his wife. They say the Princess refused to speak to anybody and immured herself in her bedchamber, day and night alike. For a long time, she was without the taste of food, and sleep would not visit her eyes for many a week. But today— nobody knows why— she came out and asked her maid to prepare her favourite food. Not only that. She also asked the maid to make ready her best clothes and further bade her get someone who was good at plaiting hair. The rumour continues that, after having her hair plaited and her hunger appeased, the Princess had a bath and dressed as though attending a feast. She went into her bedchamber and locked herself up. Then was the time she put a noose about her neck, bidding farewell to this world of the living. A few moments later, the King's wife came and knocked at the door to call her daughter out, but nobody answered. Thinking her daughter was merely savouring the sweet food of sleep, she ceased knocking and went away to come back later. But when she came back the second time and knocked and yet nobody answered, she became forthwith frantic and by force threw the door open. And— alas— thereupon she saw the lifeless body of the Princess suspended at the end of a rope.

FIRST CHIEF *(sighing)*: A sorry tale!

SECOND CHIEF: Horrible to hear!

THIRD CHIEF: The Princess herself knows why she took her own life.

FOURTH CHIEF: If it is true that she was with child, what other reason could be there than that for her suicide?

(Enter TUTU and BOTA from the palace.)

TUTU: Alas for me! I am undone! My happiness...my happiness is gone! Peace has fled from me! Everything has been taken away! Pitiless grows the ire of the gods against me... Today is a day of gloominess! A day of bitterness! My only daughter... my only child... the centre of my world... has been taken away!

BOTA: Show yourself a man, my King.

TUTU (*ignoring him*): Now scarcely will I desire to be among the living; for I have become like a disembodied spirit. Henceforward Tutu is a dead man; his life is living death. Oh, how do I tell my story? When Sasabonsam is down on the ground people say he is a wizard; how much more when he has settled himself on top of an *odum* tree, and that *odum* tree is also bearing tailless monkeys as its fruit? Oh, I am adrift in my canoe, and the wind rebels against me! It rebels against me.

BOTA: Show yourself a man, my King.

TUTU (*eyeing him steadily*): Is it not easy for you to let those words fall from your mouth? Tell me, what can cause one a greater pain than this? The only seed I planted in a woman's womb— gone!

CHIEFS: Our condolences to your Majesty.

TUTU (*unheeding*): I am dead, oh, I am dead!

SECOND CHIEF: Take heart, your Majesty.

TUTU: Where are you, my Chiefs? The men who help me govern this land— where are you?

CHIEFS: We are here, your Majesty.

TUTU: Can I ask you to do something for me?

CHIEFS: We stand ready to fulfil your Majesty's commands.

TUTU: Pray go inside and prepare my daughter's body for burial. Do that with speed, I beseech you. I want her body committed to earth without delay.

CHIEFS: It shall be as your Majesty has bidden.

(Exeunt CHIEFS.)

BOTA: What would my King have me do?

TUTU: Stay with me, Bota. Do stay with me, for I fear a fear.

BOTA: What fear, my King?

TUTU: Oh, I fear… I fear that I am the cause of my daughter's death. *(Nodding sorrowfully)*I fear that that poor girl put a noose about her neck because of me. How that prospect torments my breast! I have become entangled in a web of dread, Bota. Oh, why did I do it? Why did I drive her to kill herself?

BOTA: It is all in the mind, my King.

TUTU *(with thinly veiled anger)*: Is it?

BOTA: How can you blame yourself for your daughter's suicide? Only the gods know why she did that to herself.

TUTU *(thundering)*: None of your lip, fellow! Cease this your 'spider' ways of reasoning! I will not allow you to deceive me… not for a single moment!

BOTA: I have always walked with your Majesty in all good conscience.

TUTU *(menacingly)*: Then, for once, allow me to form my own thoughts. Allow me to use my own brain for once!

BOTA: Pardon me, my King, if I have been a bad influence on you.

(Enter GUARD from offstage.)

GUARD: The Priest of Tano is here to see your Majesty.

TUTU *(surprised)*: The Priest of Tano?

GUARD: Yes, your Majesty.

TUTU: Is he alone?

GUARD: Yes, he is, your Majesty.

TUTU: Hurry your steps and ask him in!

GUARD: I obey your Majesty.

(Exit **GUARD.***)*

TUTU *(pleased)*: Oho! Bad tidings are swift-winged birds. The Priest of Tano has heard about my daughter's death and he is here to offer his condolences.

BOTA *(affectedly reassuring)*: Without question, the people venerate you, my King. Your sorrow is their sorrow, your joy their joy.

TUTU: Upon my word, nothing could be further from the truth!

BOTA: It's true, my master. You are their King— something of a god in their estimation.

(Enter **TANO.** *As in the Second Act, he is now clad in the clothes of a priest and carries a staff.)*

TUTU *(with passion)*: Aged mouthpiece of the gods, much obliged am I for your coming. My daughter— my princess— the only fruit of my loin— is now dead and gone. She put a noose about her neck, and presently my Chiefs are in there preparing her body for burial. Now that you are here, I know you shall pray for the peaceful repose of her soul for me.

TANO *(the voice of iron)*: Don't think I have come to mourn the dead, young man. Death's sickle doesn't reap one place alone. Upon my lips I bear a message from the gods to you— a message not to be made light of.

TUTU *(elegiac)*: Oh, a message! *(Sighs.)* Speak, mighty One, I am all ears.

TANO: Before taking her own life, your daughter put a curse on the man who uncovered her nakedness and made her pregnant. This curse has come upon you.

BOTA: What?

TUTU *(flabbergasted)*: What are you saying, mighty One? My daughter was pregnant before her death? And she

124

cursed the man responsible for the pregnancy? And the curse is on me?

TANO: And there is only one way of neutralizing the effect of that curse. That is, you shall not shed tears over her death, for if you do so, you shall go mad and lose all that you possess.

TUTU *(wryly)*: I deserve that, don't I?

TANO: The frowning face of a goat will not prevent it from being taken to the slaughterhouse, young man. If you disobey the gods, your end shall come. You shall go mad and lose your throne and crown. I say again, the gods must not be disobeyed. Now, pray, I take leave of you.

(Exit **TANO.***)*

TUTU *(turning towards the household shrine)*: O you deathless Ones called gods, from whose eyes nothing evil can be hidden, who is a mortal man to deceive you? Who is he born of a woman to throw dust in your eyes? Do you see him as your equal, this creature who is a debtor to death? Do you see him as your peer? Then you are mistaken, deathless Ones. Take your eyes off him, for he is human. Cease giving him your attention, for he is unlike you. Nine months spent he in the belly of a woman before seeing light of day. And like the beast of the field, he grows weary, sickens, and does nothing save eating and drinking. What will befall him even in the nearest future, he doesn't know. How his days on earth shall be extinguished, he doesn't have the slightest idea. A weakling is he, this bag of flesh and bones— no stronger than a reed in a gale. As a bird flaps its wings unceasingly until it loses all its feathers, even in such wise wastes he all his strength and becomes a target for the arrow of death. Then why do you contend with him, immortal Ones? Leave him be, O, leave him be!

BOTA: Compose yourself, my King. You know that man never puts a foot wrong when pronouncing the will of the gods.

TUTU: Don't mistake my bitterness for foolhardiness, good friend. This grief of mine— this incalculable grief— is too heavy for me to bear.

BOTA: That's true. But make sure you don't mourn over your daughter's death, otherwise what the priest said will come to pass.

(Enter **CHIEFS** *and* **TOWNSFOLK***, carrying Ohenewaa's body on a hammock.)*

FIRST CHIEF: We have obeyed your Majesty's behest. Now we are sending the body to the outskirts of our town to carry out what our custom demands before we bury her.

TUTU *(expressionless)*: What do you mean by that? What custom?

FIRST CHIEF: You know quite well the custom, my King. Anyone who commits suicide is denied the obsequies of a proper burial: for suicide is an offence against Mother Earth. Therefore the body of that person is sent to the outskirts of our town, where it is flogged and decapitated before being buried.

TUTU *(savagely)*: No way! I will not let you do that to my daughter! I will not let you bury her like a dog. She *is* a Princess— the daughter of a great King. Is an elephant skinned on a palm leaf even if it is thin? I don't care about your barbaric custom. You shall give my daughter her due rite of burial— I insist!

SECOND CHIEF: Don't be angry, your Majesty. For we cannot transgress the tradition of our land. This custom has been observed since time immemorial, you know that. And you do indeed well know that if we fail to observe it, even Mother Earth, mother of all creation, will not open her bosom to contain your daughter's grave.

TUTU: You are mad, my friend. You've lost your senses. Do you think I will let you put me to shame? If so, you need your heads examined. I have seen all of you— all of you. The evil you have designed for me will upon your own heads return. You can't contend with me, for I am your King: my word is final in the affairs of state. And it shall be as I have said.

THIRD CHIEF: Pray stop this, your Majesty. It is unseemly for a King to oppose the laws of his own land.

TUTU *(a sour smile)*: Aahh! Teach me about your laws! Teach me about your customs!

THIRD CHIEF: Your Majesty—

TUTU *(facing them)*: I say, those of you who desire my hurt— your evil machinations will come to naught. I'll show you that I am the dread lion. No-one plays with my tail.

FOURTH CHIEF: So what does your Majesty want us to do now?

TUTU: What I have said I have said. You shall give my daughter her due rite of burial. *(Raises his hand heavenwards to swear)*And any man who dares infringe my command shall see his death.

(He goes into the palace.)

FOURTH CHIEF: This is very bad! Very, very bad. I expected as much.

FIRST CHIEF: He calls our custom "barbaric", forgetting that it is the same custom that made him King.

FOURTH CHIEF: The saying is true, brothers: Even if the goat changes into a sheep, there will always be a patch of black somewhere.

SECOND CHIEF: What do we do now?

FIRST CHIEF: What's there to be done? We cannot defy his command, for he is our King. Neither can we go contrary to that which custom dictates must be done. Perhaps we need to go to our homes and mind our own businesses.

THIRD CHIEF: No, brothers. Let us wait a little; perchance he will have a change of heart.

SECOND CHIEF: And if he doesn't…?

THIRD CHIEF: Then we leave the body to him. If he wants to eat it, we allow him to eat it. After all, it is his own daughter.

FOURTH CHIEF: If I may say so, brothers, I think we must go to our homes. As it stands now, nothing can we do to please that man in his melancholy madness.

(Cries of lamentation offstage.)

SECOND CHIEF: What is that sound I hear?

FIRST CITIZEN: I think it is the King's wife and women of the palace. They are coming to mourn the dead Princess.

FOURTH CHIEF: Pray, brothers, let us speak to Obiyaa—Without question, what she is going through is a real test of strength. Let's advice and hearten her with gentle words.

*(Enter **OBIYAA** and a group of women from the palace, all clad in black. They go round Ohenewaa's body as they mourn her.)*

OBIYAA: Can this be my destiny, Obiyaa,

Obiyaa of whom the world is weary?

Can this be that which I proposed to my Creator

before entering my mother's womb?

It is now the same with me even as with

a bird in the tight grasp of a trap.

Hapless— yes, hapless and flightless!

None to hear my doleful cry.
The arrows of sorrow were aimed at my breast
and— alas!— none of them missed the mark.
Is it not better to come and go sightless,
than to be blessed with sight and a light,
and see the light snuffed out?
O why, O why?
Why am I this unlucky?
Now my world is dark, pitch dark;
Whither I go, I do not know.
Ohenewaa, my solace, my pride, my light!
Look behind you before you go.
Look round the world you are leaving behind.
Did you spare a thought for me?
Or did you smile when subjecting me
to this dire torment?
How cruel of you, Ohenewaa!
How un-childish of you, my child!
I will not curse you; no, I will not:
Fare you well in the land of the dead!

(She kneels beside the body and sheds more tears.)

FIRST CHIEF: Destiny has been false to you, my dear daughter. But now contain yourself and weep no more. It is the Supreme Being that pounds fufu for the one-armed man. Weep no more; all shall be well again.

SECOND CHIEF: Pray cease tears, virtuous wife of our King. Stop crying and be of good cheer. Need I say, no matter how long the moon disappears, someday it must shine again.

THIRD CHIEF: We all feel sick at heart about your daughter's death. It is something that bewilders us all.

OBIYAA *(holding the corpse tightly)*: Ah! Ah! Ah! My world is now dark. My sun has been blotted out.

FOURTH CHIEF: May you never be forlorn by this terrible loss, my lady. May the gods wipe away all your tears.

(The bodyguards restrain her from the body and the palace women console her.)

Scene 4

(CHIEFS and Townsfolk are still waiting before the palace; Ohenewaa's body left alone. OBIYAA is sobbing silently.)

SECOND CHIEF: I don't know why the King is still not coming out. Look at the face of the sky: shades of evening will soon envelop us.

THIRD CHIEF: Somebody must go and speak to him. He must give us word-of-leave to send the body away.

FOURTH CHIEF: So say I too. Somebody must go and speak to him.

FIRST CHIEF: When an old woman goes to fetch water, we know she will certainly come back; but it is how long she will be at it we want to know. We can send somebody to go and talk to him right now, but what remains to be told is if he will give in.

THIRD CHIEF: Why not send what's his name here?

TOWNSFOLK *(variously)*: Yes, send Bota! Send Bota!

FOURTH CHIEF: It seems everybody wants us to send Bota and I think what they are saying is right. Bota is the only person he listens to in this town.

THIRD CHIEF: Come now, Bota. We beg you to go and speak to your friend for us. Ask him to give us leave to send the body away and comply with custom.

BOTA: My lords, I would gladly do what you ask of me. But as it stands now, my master is full of wrath. And you know his wrath is a raging fire that consumes all that comes its way. I suggest that we wait for some time, for his wrath to subside.

(Enter GUARD, running.)

FIRST CHIEF: Why do you come here in such speed, servant of the King? What is pursuing you?

GUARD: I am a bearer of ill tidings, my lords. What I've seen with my eyes is too heavy for my mouth.

FIRST CHIEF: What is it? Tell forth what you have seen.

GUARD: People of our land—

CHIEFS: Yes?

GUARD: The King has gone mad.

ALL: What!

GUARD: The King… he has gone mad. And he wants to kill me! He is coming with a machete.

SECOND CHIEF: Get yourself not into trouble, young man. Know you are speaking of the supreme lord of the land.

GUARD: I dare not make fun of the King, my good lord. I would never get myself into trouble by an ungoverned tongue.

FIRST CHIEF: Take your time, my son, and tell us— Tell us what has happened.

GUARD: My lords, I was with the King in his bedchamber, keeping his person and standing ready to do his bidding. For a long time, he sat stiff-stricken on his bed and said nothing to me. He just sat and groundward bowed he his head, every now and again smiting his breast and restraining his eyes from tears. Then, abruptly, it burst from his lips, "Will she ever forgive me?" I didn't have the slightest inkling of what he was talking about, and so I asked, "Has your Majesty offended anybody?" But he didn't answer me, and asked again, "Will she ever forgive me?" Now it occurred to me that it would seem a sign of disrespect on my part if I answered the King's question again with a question. Therefore I said, "She has already forgiven your Majesty", thinking he would find solace in my words. But scarcely were those words out of my mouth when he burst into tears, wailing piteously like a woman and asking pardon from the deceased Princess. In utter bewilderment not unmingled with fear, I observed him steadily while I prayed inside my head to the gods. He wept for a long time, calling down curses upon himself and still smiting his hand upon his breast. Then, all of a sudden, he ceased the tears and let out a frightful yell. I thought it was all part of his lamentation, and so I saw nothing coming. But he uttered a second terrible yell and— alas— started tearing apart his clothes. He then took a machete and, threatening to hack me into pieces, chased me out of the royal bedchamber. That was the time saw you me fleeing here, my lords. I cannot speak falsely of the King.

SECOND CHIEF: Oh, what's happening in this palace? What have we done to arouse the ire of the gods?

FIRST CHIEF: A thing like this we never saw or heard. Something must be done before it gets too late.

FOURTH CHIEF: Today is an evil day. The sky even made it clear this morning.

FIRST CHIEF *(to* **GUARD***)*: Now, young man, go quickly and fetch the Priest of Tano. Tell him the King needs him as a matter of urgency.

GUARD: I obey my lord.

(Exit.)

FIRST CHIEF: I am very certain Tano's priest shall be able to help him. I mean, can anything be beyond the wit of that man?

SECOND CHIEF: Absolutely not! He is the priest of a most powerful deity.

THIRD CHIEF: The tale of the servant is true. I see the King coming here and— alas— he is half-naked!

(Enter **TUTU***, scantily clad and wielding a machete. It is abundantly clear to us that he is now mad. As soon as* **OBIYAA** *sees him, she collapses.)*

TUTU *(imperturbable)*: The mountains are calling me. I will go. Oh, I will go! The fish— they are crying in the soup!

(Stops, turns, listens.)

The storm is coming!... The storm is coming!...The fire will burn the farm. I will go for my hoe. The sun is dark. O the mountains!

FIRST CHIEF: What is the matter, my King? What is the matter with you?

TUTU: Do you not hear the mountains? They are calling me.

FIRST CHIEF: Which mountains?

TUTU: The mountains in the forest. They are calling— calling me.

FIRST CHIEF: To do what?

TUTU: "To do what"? Look— this is a machete. I am taking it to the mountains. I am going to the mountains.

FIRST CHIEF *(approaching him)*: No, my King. Pray give me the machete—

TUTU *(raises machete; shouting)*: Go back or I will kill you! I will use my machete to kill you! Go back!

(Out of fear, FIRST CHIEF draws back.)

THIRD CHIEF: O gods of our land, wake up if you are asleep! What is happening to our King?

TUTU *(as before)*: The fish… they are on the mountains. Their fingers are swollen in the soup. The storm is coming into the soup.

FOURTH CHIEF: Now stop it, your Majesty.

TUTU: What?

FOURTH CHIEF: I said stop what you are doing.

TUTU: The storm?

FOURTH CHIEF: Your talk about mountains and soup.

TUTU: They are calling me. You hear them, too? You hear them, too?

FOURTH CHIEF: No, I don't. But pray give me your machete and let us go inside.

TUTU *(as before)*: They are calling me… I shall go.

FOURTH CHIEF: I know they are calling you— but ignore them. They are not real. Come and let us go into the palace.

TUTU: No, I am going to the mountains. I am going to burn the farm. The fish are in the soup. They are crying.

(He sits down on the ground and stands up. He brandishes the machete in the air. Sits down again and stands up. Brandishes the machete again.)

SECOND CHIEF: Our dear King, what is this you are doing? Do you not see we are surrounded by the whole world?

TUTU *(as before)*: The whole world… The whole mountains… The goat is sick in the soup. The fire will burn the farm. I must go. The sun is dark and my clothes are dirty. I must go to the mountains— my clothes are dirty…the time has come for the goat to be in the soup. Do you see my clothes? Travel-worn. Here— let me remove it.

(He holds his undergarment in an attempt to remove it; CHIEFS rush forward to stop him.)

CHIEFS: Pray stop, your Majesty!

TUTU *(machete raised. threatening as before)*: Go back or I will kill you! I will kill all of you!

SECOND CHIEF: Do not remove your undergarment, your Majesty. Pray stop humiliating yourself and the throne of the land.

TUTU: If you don't go back, I will kill all of you! Come no closer! Come no closer!

135

(CHIEFS *shrink backwards in fright. Enter* **TANO** *and* **GUARD**.)

FIRST CHIEF: Oh, how glad we are of your coming, companion of the gods! Look at the King— we do not know what is happening to him. He is behaving quite strangely today, disgracing the throne in front of the whole world.

SECOND CHIEF: Pray do something for us, mighty One. Speak to the gods for us, we beseech you.

TANO: Let no man speak against the gods for what is now happening; for they are infallible in all their ways.

FIRST CHIEF: We know that perfectly well, mighty One. We know that the gods are just and will not let go unpunished any misdeed. But speak to them for us.

TANO *(stoutly)*: Be it known to all of you here that this man you see…this your king…has only himself to thank for what you all see today. He committed an odious crime. He carried out an object of divine abhorrence, and now the gods are punishing him for it.

FIRST CHIEF: Tell us if we deserve to know. What did he do to merit such a punishment?

TANO *(Without a change of tone)*: Your King murdered his own brother by luring him to drink poisoned palm wine.

ALL *(surprised; shouting)*: What!

TANO: He coveted his brother's throne and crown, and sent him to an early grave on that account. But after the murder, the gods, as retribution for that abomination, gave Tutu the alternative of either sleeping with his own daughter or being struck dead upon seeing his brother's ghost. He chose to sleep with his own daughter and was able to do so by administering a sleep-inducing potion into food for her. But four months afterwards, his daughter found out that she was with child and yet did not know who had lain with her.

Upon discovering it, the girl cursed the man who impregnated her, and afterwards took her own life. What you see today is the effect of the curse Ohenewaa laid upon her own father. The mighty gods are just, let no-one blame them.

ALL: Ei! Indeed this world is dark!

FIRST WOMAN: So is it Tutu who murdered King Okokroko? Never would have guessed!

SECOND WOMAN: I will never trust any person on this earth! Not even my own husband.

FIRST CHIEF *(after a pause)*: To what conclusion can we come, brothers and sisters? The King deserves what he has got, doesn't he?

TOWNSFOLK: Absolutely!

FIRST CHIEF: The gods have spoken; they administer justice. They bless him who needs to be blessed and punish him who needs to be punished.

*(*BOTA *comes forward.)*

BOTA: Be pleased to answer my question for me, mighty One.

TANO: What is it?

BOTA: Is there nothing we can do to placate the gods so as to reverse this punishment? Something to help the King regain his sanity?

TANO: No, nothing!

BOTA: You mean, nothing?

TANO: None whatsoever.

BOTA *(shaking his head)*: No, mighty One, there must be a way. There must be something we can do— sacrifices, libation, or anything of such a kind. My friend can never go mad like this… *(Turns to* **TUTU.***)*

> Adu Tutu, the deep-bosomed river that
> overflows its banks in dry season!

TUTU: What?

BOTA: Adu Tutu, the firm-fixed whetstone that
eats fresh iron before sleeping!

TUTU: Who are you?

BOTA: Adu Tutu, the mighty crab
that knows where the alluvial gold is found!
It is you I call, my master.
Pray tell me, Adu Tutu:
What fell from the sky and cut the tendril,
preventing the yam from increasing?
What possessed the fetish priest
and made him a victim on the altar
of his own fetishes?
Did we not whip ourselves up into a frenzy
playing the sacred drums for them?
Or is your soul an unlucky one,
causing you to fall into the hands of a legion?
When a ghost offers you his hand for greeting,
Adu Tutu, you draw yours back.
This greeting is a greeting of death;
pray draw your hand back.
Now all the mice are looking on, smiling,
waiting for the cat to cease clinging to life.
Put them to shame, great one,
put them to shame.

(He advances a couple of steps towards his friend.)
Adu Tutu,
my master,
my brother,
my friend.

TUTU: What? *(Violently)*Come no closer! Come no closer!

BOTA: Pray give me the machete, my master. Give it to me… put all the enemies to shame and give me the machete. They say there is nothing we can do about your situation. But doubtless, they merely want to see your downfall. Put them to shame. Here— hand it over. Hand the machete over.

(TUTU now seems stupefied, staring at BOTA and muttering to himself. BOTA slowly takes hold of the machete and removes it from his friend's hand. The two embrace and the crowd clap in admiration. They are impressed by the power of friendship. But suddenly, TUTU grabs the machete back and, without a moment's hesitation, thrusts it into his friend's belly. The entire crowd, with the exception of TANO, runs pell-mell for their lives, leaving BOTA dying in a pool of blood.)

BOTA *(groaning)*: Oh, my King, my King… you… have… killed… me!
(He dies.)

TUTU: I have killed him! I have killed him! With my weapon… I have killed him! Now I will go to the mountains. I will go. The fish… they are calling me from the soup. The storm is coming. Oh, the storm is coming!

(He runs off the stage, leaving behind his land and his kingdom. TANO turns to face the audience, smiling…knowingly)

TANO: Is it not wrong for mortal men to say that the end of a thing is better than its beginning? The question is, can there be an end without a beginning? Can there be the death of a thing if the birth thereof has not already taken place? What was, what is, and what is yet to be for man, does or did happen to him through the doings of his own hands.

Yes— as he sows today, even so shall he reap tomorrow. The end is no better than the beginning; neither is the beginning better than the end.

(As he goes off, the lights fade and the talking drum bids us goodnight)

CURTAIN DESCENDS SLOWLY.

THE END

Printed in the United States
By Bookmasters